CW01338136

TRIUMPH HOUSE
Poetry with a Purpose

CHRISTIAN MINDS

Edited by

Natalie Nightingale

First published in Great Britain in 2001 by
TRIUMPH HOUSE
Remus House,
Coltsfoot Drive,
Peterborough, PE2 9JX
Telephone (01733) 898102

All Rights Reserved

Copyright Contributors 2001

HB ISBN 1 86161 963 4
SB ISBN 1 86161 968 5

FOREWORD

For many of us the medium of poetry offers us a voice - a voice to speak out and let others know what we feel, think and desire. It is the vital bridge of communication that lets us share our innermost thoughts and messages on life to people who may need that vital surge of poetic inspiration. It offers experience to those with none or little, spreads light to those in darkness and at the same time it encourages others that they are not alone. *Christian Minds* is a unique collection of poetry written in a variety of styles and on a combination of themes. The poems are easy to relate to and encouraging to read, offering engaging entertainment to their reader.

This delightful collection is sure to win your heart, making it a companion for life and perhaps even earning that favourite little spot upon your bookshelf.

Natalie Nightingale
Editor

CONTENTS

Daughter Of Eve	Nina Haime	1
Snowflakes In The Sky	Annie Overy	2
Destiny's Child (I Have A Son In Australia)	Nigel Gatiss	3
Jesus I Believe	Paul Walker	4
Merry-Go-Round	Amy Elizabeth Holland	5
Friends And Neighbours	Heather Breadnam	6
Ellis Park	Desiree Knoesen	7
By My Daughter's Bed	Chrissi	8
Gag Writer	Robert D Shooter	9
A Little Piece Of Heaven	Jim Cuthbert	10
Autumn Then	Marion Schoeberlein	11
Dear Child . . .	Samantha Drewry	12
Sunday	John G Woods	14
Our Home Is Heaven	Wendy Joiner	15
Good Shepherd	Helen Owen	16
Nature's Day	Derek Pile	17
Butterflies	Carmel Wright	18
Triple Joy	Sheila Walters	19
Titanic	Emmanuel Petrakis	20
Lebanon	F McFaul	21
Come Out On Top	Anthony Higgins	22
Sleeping Beauty	D Wilkinson	23
Dreams And Wishes	Keith Allison	24
Foot And Mouth	Christa Todd	26
Dry Your Tears	Z Cole	27
A Child Is Born	E Corr	28
Sacred Heart	Josephine Foreman	29
Out Of The Darkness	Colin Allsop	30
Fools	Don Goodwin	31
Ending Is Beginning	Kieran Brogan	32
A Mortal Ascension	C Thornton	34
Sonnet for The Millennium	Sheila Burnett	35
Full Circle	Gladys C'Ailceta	36
The Song Of Space	Stephen Gyles	37
George And I	Pamela Earl	38

Sin Poured Scorn	Joyce A W Arnold	39
The Miracle	Claire Bloomfield	40
Dark And Shadow	Robert Robb	42
Why Go To Church?	Cathy Mearman	43
Keeper Of My Heart	Carol Olson	44
The Christ	R P Scannell	45
Lord . . . You!	Richard D Reddell	46
Remember	Matthew L Burns	47
Be Thankful	Margaret Findlay	48
The Baby	Muriel Johnson	49
Marriage Blessing	Perry McDaid	50
The Shepherd On The Hillside	E M Gough	51
Sacrifice	Sandy Grebby	52
Thy Kingdom Come	Ivy Lott	53
The Brothers	Alan Pow	54
A Lenten Offering	Joyce Angel	55
My Guide	Will A Tilyard	56
Such A Love As This	John Harrold	57
More Than I Can Bear	Denis Martindale	58
New Covenant	Mazard (Micky) Hunter	59
Wishing Me Blue Skies	Rowland Warambwa	60
Santa's Christmas Journey	Ernest Hannam	61
Greatness	John Gaze	62
My Prayer	C Shanks	63
My Thanks	Wendy Souter	64
Touching Hands	Mary Skelton	65
Calvary	David Reynoldson	66
Christmas 2000	Frank L Appleyard	67
Christian Friendship	Gordon W Hendry	68
In Splendour Ablaze	Jean Turner	69
Gethsemane?	Cynthia Taylor	70
Some Men	Iaian W Wade	71
The Comforter	R T James	72
Life Is A Storybook	Irene Smith	73
What Be The Point?	L J Doel	74
Endurance	Pat Melbourn	75
Burning Trails	Ian Barton	76
Spiritual Seeds	Graham Hare	77

Mary	Elizabeth Myra Crellin	78
Revelation	Amelia Michael	80
Love's First Decree	Edmund Saint George Mooney	81
My Really Good Friend	Ruth Daviat	82
Untitled	Janice Frazer	83
I Long To Be	GIG	84
Lost And Found	Henry Disney	85
The Solitary Man	Linda Beavis	86
The Best	Anne Mary McMullan	87
I Wanted ...	Andrew Sanders	88
Laughter	Reg Cook	89
God's Love	Thelma Cook	90
The Sabbath	Elaine McCulloch Smith	91
Where Are You God?	Roystone Herbert	92
Silence Of The Lambs	Brian Fisher	93
To Give Of Peace	Roger Mosedale	94
Take An Interest	N Mason	95
God's Love Reaches Out	Pamela D Jewell	96
Teaching And Preaching The Word	David Hill	97
Jesus, The Pearl Of Great Price	Elizabeth De Meza	98
The First Miracle	Sheila Burnett	99
Suffer The Little Children	Sandy Chambers	100
We Are God's Children	Kenneth Mood	102
Let This Be	Juliet Eaton	103
Why?	Mary Shovlin	104
He Is ...	Francis McFaul	105
Taking God For Granted	Marlene Devlin	106
Love From Within	Ruth Holder	107
Easter	P Wright	108
The Valley Walk	S K Clark	109
In Your Struggle	Ebenezer Essuman	110
Walk To Wonderland	Lesley Allen	111
Let Your Soul Be Free	Angela Hovell	112
Though	Nicholas Winn	113
Gradually And Gratefully	Brian Marshall	114
God Blessed Us	Ann Beard	115
The Weather	Jean C Pease	116

The Sage	Rangram Boontarig	117
Springtime	Mary Hayman	118
Maranatha! (Come Lord Jesus!)	Reverend Eddy Burfitt	119
Untitled	Philip Allen	120
Peace Be With You	Jean Dorrington	121
Whose Hand On The Tiller?	Ernest S Peaford	122
Gifts All Around	Marcella Pellow	124
Amen	H Cotterill	125
The Blooms Were There To Remind Me	Rosie Hues	126
Untitled	C D Isherwood	127
My Thanks	Amelia Roberts	128
Harborough 2999	H Griffiths	129
Easter	Doreen Day	130
The Meaning Of Spring	Kathleen M Hatton	131
The Coming Of Christ	Brenda Killingback	132
Be Still	Kathleen Potter	133
The Lord's Gift	Ann Ogilvie	134
My Daily Prayer	Joan Picton	135
Safe Home At Eventide	Mary Ferguson	136
That Better Part	Olive Bedford	137
Innocent Eyes	Susan Revell	138
A Goodnight Prayer	Elisabeth Morley	139
Live In Peace	Louise White	140
Poetic Prayers	Janet Larkin	141
Chaos	Pearls	142
On High	Hugh Campbell	143
Ever Present	T Butler	144
To You I Pray	Joan Smith	145
Sounds Of Temptation	Marlène Walker	146
Words Of Gold	John Rae Walker	147
The Reply	J B Allan	148
The Heritage	Marie Stanton	149
A Circle With No End	M A Shipp Yule	150
Psalm 121 - The Lord Our Protector	John Cook	151
Turning Around	H D Hensman	152

Lost In Wonder, Love And Praise . . .	David Varley	153
Truth's Vision`	Margaret Gurney	154
Dear Lord! Is It Me?	B Hayman	155
The Things That I See	Helen Riley	156
Music Of The Flower Garden	Nigel M Chisholm	157
Beauty Is . . .	Elizabeth Leach	158
Magical Woodland	Lynda Fordham	159
My Daughter	A F Mace	160
Things I Love In God's World	Irene Hart	161
Summer Time	Anne Greenhow	162
The Rainbow	Jane Finlayson	163
Springtime	Tom Rutherford	164
There Is A Time	Jeni Merrifield	166
Thankfulness	Julia L Holden	167
Wondrous Love	Wendy Ann Lively	168

DAUGHTER OF EVE

O yielding daughter of Eve, why allow such torment?
To give of yourself so freely and yet take little for sustenance.
You cannot live from love alone, you need to grow and flourish
Do not resign yourself to mere existence, for you are Mightier than any
Adam and healthier of heart.
Spread your crushed roots and allow yourself to expand and rise.

You suffocate yourself to allow others to breathe and prosper,
Denying them nothing which you are able to sacrifice.
Your soul is bright, lucid and pure of heart
Your branches protect all those that gather beneath them
And you shelter all those who selfishly form there.

You bear the fruits of your labour for all to feast upon and yet
You do not take any nourishment for yourself.
You permeate warmth and comfort others and yet
You do not take any warmth in comfort for yourself.

Do not wither by denying your true self,
Allow your inner strength to uplift you and allow you to bloom.
You are beautiful and beautiful things need to grow.

Nina Haime

SNOWFLAKES IN THE SKY

Crystal snowflakes in the sky,
Please shine for me this eve;
The stars and planets circling by,
Their beauty I perceive.

Please take away Earth's darkness,
And all destruction flee;
As on this cold and crispy night,
Shine on their cosmic flight.

To circle on inspiring awe,
Their light illumines Earth,
And out of darkness we implore,
The gift of life we saw.

Servants are we of this world,
Transcending from all time;
The prophecies we do unfold,
A tree of life to climb.

Our mystery of time before,
We search of books untold,
A glorious light for us to find,
Our hearts were left behind.

And even of this 'wakening,
Of truth and love inspired,
Heavens' armies are prepared,
For the new life is desired.

Annie Overy

DESTINY'S CHILD (I HAVE A SON IN AUSTRALIA)
(For Dorothy And Simon)

What heartfelt thread, drew you from these shores?
Was it fate's guided intervention;
Or the silent whispers of destiny's intentions?

And like a gypsy; were you born to roam?
A wandering, 'free spirit', an unbound angel, a soul to walk alone.

And do your streams of life, flow contained, preordained and
                                                                restrained?
Confined . . . no choice which way to go.
Like the changing phases of the moon: naturally born to ebb, and flow.

And though your words, fall softly from my lips: like a sweet
remembrance . . . of a tender kiss.
Such words are shrouded in confusion, and echoes of illusion.
Like a lover's, distant, sad refrain . . . 'just let it be, let it be, let it be;'
Its emotions are felt over; over, and over again.

And do we understand, 'those closest to us?'
How a river runs through their souls.
Its breath of dark reflective moments . . . or sunlit diamonds,
that swiftly flow.
And we accept; we cannot change:
For, 'love is love;' and we love them, just the same.
As life's breath . . . 'breathes'; 'what will be . . . will be.'
Its laws are bound in change and magic, awe and mystery.
That we are blind, and cannot see; that our soul's, 'love . . .'
Is to be free.
Free to follow its nature.
'A child of destiny'.

Nigel Gatiss

JESUS I BELIEVE

Jesus I believe
That he died for you and me
That he was born again
And now reign's forever more
He's gonna wash away all our sins
He's gonna cleanse our hearts within
He's gonna take us to God's big mansion in the sky
Jesus I believe
Great miracles and wonder I have seen
You are the gift of eternal life
You are the one through whom
All love and forgiveness we receive

Paul Walker

MERRY-GO-ROUND

Are we each individually wrapped,
into a role;
a role of fate . . .?

Do we live to experience?
Or do we live to be seen to live?
And what do we learn?
Who do we learn from?
Who is to judge when our days are long gone?

Is this piece an essence of my character?
Or just an emotion to the way I think and feel?

Do I interpret my moods from a universal
language of astrology;
That inspires those to their own sights and awareness?
Is one a listener
and another a messenger?
Who is this voice, talking with only words?
Who controls the story?

Perhaps a world that no mortal eye can see,
where something simple will answer.
Something to disconnect the circular path.
The one that repeats upon itself,
spinning on its axis.

Will I look back and laugh,
knowing all then.
Or will I be a stake of the unknown?
There's no real truth in evidence,
so we argue belief.

And do you question the same as me?
Or would you just let it be?

Amy Elizabeth Holland

FRIENDS AND NEIGHBOURS

Hello dear Jesus. Today we meet again.
The sun is up, the night sky gone, and not a sign of rain.
Most people like to eat and drink, before they leave the house.
Sometimes there is no time to stop before they leave the home.
The precious time to speak, to you has slipped away once more.
Then the time is racing by, and everything goes wrong.
Just stop and think!
And make things right Jesus, save your precious hour.
For Jesus needs our company to lead us day by day.
Without Him we are nothing in any sort of way.
So day by day, and hour by hour, we listen very hard.
The small, quiet voice of Jesus, and the whisper near my heart.
So keep the hour with Jesus and you won't get it wrong.
Feed the poor and help the wounded.
Search your hearts, and spare a room, for those that have no roof.
The Good Shepherd found the lost sheep, the one that went astray.
He put it in His loving arms, and took it home to stay.

Heather Breadnam

Ellis Park

A crowded stadium, excitement fills the crisp night air
Thousands gather, fans join together, not one empty chair
Teams have trained many hours, soccer the name of the game
Nobody dreams of the nightmare ahead, history repeats itself again.

Too many people, too little space, barricades bar the way
Bribes are offered, money accepted, yet no one's about to stay
Mayhem erupts, panic spreads, fear grips the human heart
Holding hands, terror takes its toll, loved ones are torn apart.

Without any warning devastation strikes - try to count the cost
Tears flow, loyalties grow, families grieve for members lost
God-fearing South Africans mourn - though we all weren't there
The aftermath of this tragic event is far too sad to bear.

Almighty God, You loved the world so You sacrificed Your Son
You understand the heart of man please comfort, console each one
Lord Jesus You died for us to live yet, sadness is all around
Teach us mortals to accept Your Word, then peace will soon be found
O Holy Spirit though death has come, help us believe the Gospel story
Please heal those wounds, dry those tears, touch each soul with God's
grace and glory.

Desiree Knoesen

BY MY DAUGHTER'S BED

As I lay her down to sleep
I pray the angels her soul to keep.
I lay her gently and stroke her hair,
While she sleeps without a care.
As I watch her while she breathes,
I ask God to protect her - please.
Her long blond hair reflects the light.
Her faultlessness is a mother's delight.
I pull up the covers and tuck her in -
This is where my prayers begin.

Dear Father,
I ask of you, this night to watch
And send an angel down to touch
Our dreams, our wishes and our prayer
So we'll sleep safely in your care.
My Lord you know that we will serve
You all the while we're on this earth.
I ask you to guide us down the paths
And keep our faith within our grasp.
I ask you Father if I may,
These small requests whenever I pray.
Thank you Lord for being there
To hear me when I am in prayer.
Amen.

Chrissi

GAG WRITER
(To Chris Burden)

Laughter of Abraham at God
that he'd be a father with Sarah
did He just not understand the obstacles?
Never mind of a great nation.

Laughter of Sarah at herself
knowing her barrenness
and Abraham's alleged prowess elsewhere
but also at God for His naiveté
that He could even think Abraham would
and especially at His thinking she'd let him
or even if she did that they could.

Yet the last laugh of all
whether derisory or loving
or could it be both at the same time?
Was God's, where Izaak was born.

Robert D Shooter

A Little Piece Of Heaven

There's a little piece of heaven, in
the street where I live, where the gates
are always open wide, and always there's
a welcome, that's warm and full of love,
where together peace and happiness abide,

for there to greet me is an angel, no beauty
can compare, who wears a crown of silver
tinged with gold, her smile would shame a
sunbeam, her eyes would light the dawn, and
her face where only in dreams you would behold,

together we walk her garden, a paradise she made,
where all the colours of the world fill the eye,
where we sometimes sit and listen to the music
of the birds, and taste the perfume of a sunset
drifting by,

then in the twilight of the evenings, as the
shadows softly fall, I sit and count my blessings
there to see, then I close my eyes, and thank my
God, for this piece of heaven here on earth, and
for the angel he sent here just for me.

Jim Cuthbert

AUTUMN THEN

Chrysanthemums were sitting
Where summer flowers had been,
Rain was sadder and I knew
That it was autumn then.

A different God was in
The sky and every tree,
I knew that He was making
Autumn again for me.

Marion Schoeberlein

DEAR CHILD...

I love you in so many ways
let me tell you how much I love you . . .
I created the earth
and filled it with life
that you could eat and drink
be fruitful and multiply.
I loved you so much
that I gave you a choice
to choose between good and evil
life or death
and you chose what I hated
and even though you broke my heart
I still loved you
I knew this would happen
and yet in my love
I made another way
that you could come back to me.
I love my son
we have been together before the beginning of time
and He became my gift of love to you.
In my love I gave you Jesus
I gave and keep giving you a choice
between good and evil
life or death in him
and Jesus prays that you would
choose life in Him and not death in the world
I love you so much
and I will keep loving you back into my arms
like it was in the beginning
in our beautiful Garden of Eden.

W a i t in g

W orshipping God, being
A mazed at the
I ntimate relationship overflowing with
T reasures from above, blessings that unfold with
I nspiration, wisdom, knowledge and a
N eed to know
G od more and more.

Samantha Drewry

SUNDAY

Today is resurrection;
Love risen
From the prison -
From death,
New life's breath.
New vision now given,
Dejection driven
Away.

Growing cold?
Growing old?
Today lives.
God gives
Soft wind
Soul-refreshing rain,
Today's spark, healing sun,
Joy again -
New day
Begun.

However late
No need to wait:
Enter life's gateway
This Sunday.

John G Woods

OUR HOME IS HEAVEN

When snowflakes are a falling
And frost is sparkling bright
The warm glow from the windows
Smiles a welcome to the night
We'll sit beside an old log fire
Our hearts will be content
We have our little cottage
And know it's heaven-scent
So with flowers in the garden
And roses round the door
We'll live our lives in happiness
And couldn't wish for more.

Wendy Joiner

GOOD SHEPHERD

Of the sweet white lamb
That wanders far
From every land
Please shine your light
All through the night
So I may find
My way home.

Helen Owen

NATURE'S DAY

Solitary snowdrops,
Soldiers of spring,
Signalling new life
Nature will bring.

Buds breaking cover
From winter's dark shroud,
Birds heralding new beginnings
Singing out loud.

Air of virgin freshness
Season of new hope,
Furnishing inspiration
Good reason to cope.

Savour the new birth
Awakening from its rest,
Nature at its purest
Life's simple best

Derek Pile

BUTTERFLIES

Today I chased a fleeting, flimsy dream
A tiny fragile thing of gossamer
I tried to catch a multicoloured butterfly
To feel it flutter in my hands
I even traced a rainbow to its end
And held a million silver hopes
And dreams up high.

Last night I stretched and reached above
To touch a million stars
Bejewelled in my sky
Today the stars have gone
The sky is metal grey
The tiny coloured butterfly
Is cold and still
My cheeks are wet
With thoughts of you.

Carmel Wright

TRIPLE JOY

My sister-in-law said to me,
In a few month's time you're to be,
An auntie, would you like, two or three?
How nice to have nephews or niece,
What a surprise, 'a three piece'!
The babies were born on Valentine's day,
Auntie and uncle had gone away.
We got this note announcing 'a birth',
Not according to sister-in-law's girth,
Whose phone call confirmed three!
Those nephews we were about to see,
And will never forget our first view
Of our triplet nephews in SCBU.

Greg was eldest by minutes few,
His weight when born was 3lb 10oz.
Another three minutes passed then,
Aaron was born at 3lb 8oz.
As Dad was told to sit and wait,
Ross appeared weighing 2lb 9oz,
Babies' Mum and Dad were fine!

Our nephews born on Valentine's day,
Will soon be *nine,* 'growing away',
Some may wonder, how do they cope?
We have the answer, no time to 'mope',
For more enjoyment we could not hope.

(SCBU - Special Care Baby Unit.)

Sheila Walters

TITANIC

O spirit of Man, rising and heaving,
Your own fate shaping and weaving,
From caveman to God-man, your urges swell,
Gushing from Mind, that bottomless well,
Where sleeping giants grunt at night,
Slowly to wake to a shaft of light,
Heaving through oceans, uncharted seas,
Thoughts made of steel defying the breeze;
The heavens may rumble, the heavens may roar,
You've mastered the tempest and mastered the shore
You've split up the atom, you've mastered the sky,
Why, O little man, pray tell me why?

Emmanuel Petrakis

LEBANON

There is not enough cattle in Lebanon
   the book of Isaiah says
      for burnt offerings unto the Lord
         mercy, not sacrifice He desires

There is not enough cattle in Britain now
   no matter how high the fires burn
      to appease the false deity commerce
         to the Father again we must turn

           the lamb, the ewe, the ram, the sow
           the boar, the bull, the calf, the cow
           the man, the nation, the cull, must bow
           and turn unto the Lord

Lebanon is not sufficient for altar fires
and its animals are not enough
to stem the tide that breaks upon our shore
extend mercy, o please, Lord of love

F McFaul

COME OUT ON TOP

When everything seems to fall apart
Don't lose heart
Believe me, all will change around
Be back on the ground
Love is a funny thing
Things alter in spring
Say you don't know
Rain, sunshine or snow
Often when you sneeze
Particles float in the breeze
Feelings falter from day to day
Come what may
No matter what pain you're in
Needle point or pin
Remember you're not alone
Strengthen that backbone
Some come unstuck
That's their bad luck
Be pliable
You're totally reliable

Anthony Higgins

SLEEPING BEAUTY

Awakened by an apparition!
A radiant vision
Shone forth
Out of the twisted sea of wept in blankets
Her face now dry
A tender look, so forlorn -
Innocence restored
Her sheer beauty stunned me
Stirred my very soul
Transfixed, no thought of touch
Petrified I shatter
This vision of such purity
Breathless I gazed in awe
At my living Bottichelli
Fresh and growing younger
With each virgin dawn!
Gently she turns into the pillow -
My Madonna has melted!
For the moment,
Until she wakes!

D Wilkinson

DREAMS AND WISHES

Your dreams are all wishes, they tell me,
Your dreams are all wishes, they say,
Your dreams are all wishes, my friends will insist,
But they can't take life's problems away.

Without dreams our lives would seem empty,
A gaping void we would soon find,
For our dreams not only look forwards,
But often take swift peeps behind.

It's true that some dreamers are hazy
About what they do or they say,
When dreaming of their joys and sorrows,
But that, I suppose, is their way.

Now what about hard hearts, as some are,
Who have water, not blood, in their veins,
Who scoff we see only the future,
For amassing of temporal gains?

Let them scoff, for their lives must be empty,
Devoid of all concern and care,
They can't tell a dream from a nightmare,
And have no love left over to spare

For joy often comes with our dreaming,
And pleasure is not far away,
When we just close our eyes and imagine
That life once again becomes gay.

No, don't let the scoffers deride you,
With their frowns and their glares and their sighs,
You know what's important in your life,
While they do no more than surmise.

May your dreams be more blissful than ever,
May your joy affect all at your side,
Let your dreams be a bright light before you,
And love your infallible guide.

Keith Allison

FOOT AND MOUTH

How sad to walk,
through fields of green,
with no cows or sheep,
to be seen.
A lonely farmer,
with tears in his eyes,
pats his dog, by his side.
His old friend looks at him with love,
together they pray for help from above . . .

Christa Todd

DRY YOUR TEARS

Dry your tears, please don't weep,
Mourn for me not, I do not sleep.
I am in the warm summer breeze,
I'm in the new spring growth of pale green leaves.
I'm in the gentle waves lapping the shore,
I am the one who's gone on before.
I'm in the stillness of a new dawn,
I'm in a field of golden corn.
I'm the brightest star that shines in the night,
I'm in the early morning light.
I'll stay with you till the end of time,
I am yours and you are mine.
Dry your tears, please don't cry,
Mourn for me not, I did not die.

Z Cole

A Child Is Born

Young and foolish, a child is born
Pink and sweet, the end of my life
Pretence and lies, the years have gone by
Hold me close don't let me cry!

I saw her golden curls, and rosebud mouth
Pain and sorrow etched on my face
I hated myself for what I was doing
Telling myself, it was for her good,
Knowing it would save my ruin.

I held her out to him, motionless was my gaze
Did she know she was being betrayed?
I turned and left, blinded by tears
They'd never know my desperate fears.

How much does anyone wish to die?
How many times we reason why
I'll live my life with ifs and whys
Was I wrong? Will she hear my cries
Forgive me, for I'm a selfish being
When there's trouble, you see me fleeing

Life is death, and death is for meeting
A girl holds out her arms in greeting
I hold her close, seems a hundred years ago
But I have her now, and I'll never let her go.

E Corr

SACRED HEART

Sacred heart thou' be with me
As I recall days of glee
When every dawn
Our hearts were warm
Come the morning light
We always felt bright

A heavy feeling fills my heart
The way we did part
But through the mist
I remain with bliss
Given by the 'Almighty'
As one will agree

I still feel the sadness
And some loneliness
How I had to leave you alone
Whilst the doctor I did 'phone
Who abusively shouted *'I'm busy!'*
Leaving me confused

Which alone I had to endure
But - close was the 'Almighty' to 'cure'
Suddenly, you were gone!
I felt rather forlorn
And left in doubt
When barely cold the 'Doc' hustled you out!

As you lay
I thought 'Why treated this way?'
Apparently no isolated case
As others similar face
Hence this poem to 'bless'
And offer those like-wise 'caress'

Josephine Foreman

OUT OF THE DARKNESS

From the darkness came the light
The first day turned into night
The sun made way for the moon
Angels played a Holy tune
Light reflected off a cloud
As night brought forth its silent shroud

From the Father came the Son
The sadness turned into fun
On this day the first one on Earth
From heaven joy gave birth
Good was there to replace bad
Was God blessed as Jesus' Dad?

The sun was as hot as toast
With the Father was the Holy Ghost
Evil reflected off the moon
The night played the devil's tune
Everything is not black or white
Is not day just like night

Out from heaven there came hell
From perfume came sulphurs smell
Angels and demons both the same
Devil and God just like the same
Is the God in heaven above
Just a demon born of love.

Colin Allsop

Fools

If you walk with fools who say there is no God at all,
They can mock and scoff but it will all be recalled,
When you stand before the judgement throne of God who does not exist,
You will answer for all that you have done, you cannot resist,
Then you will feel the wrath of God, that you mocked for so long,
And you will then take the consequences of all you have done wrong.

Don Goodwin

Ending Is Beginning

I was sitting on the sand
I was looking out to sea
I was searching for an answer
But all I found was me

I watched a glorious sunset
Its colours lighting up the bay
As the sun said farewell
To another perfect day

But all I saw was burning red
Like the anger and the pain
Another day is dead and gone
And my life is much the same

But as the sun was sinking
Into the cool of blue
Something in me started changing
With every change in hue

Then suddenly it dawned on me
If you'll excuse the pun
Maybe that part of life is over
And a new part has begun

What if I was over there
On the other side
Sitting on the sand right now
And staring at the tide

The waves are surely breaking
The sun is surely rising
A new day is dawning
And an ending is beginning

And as the last ray of light
Danced across the swell
I felt an ease within me
And I knew that all was well.

Kieran Brogan

A Mortal Ascension

Did Dante, Milton, get it wrong? A hollow verse of empty song,
truth be known, I cannot say, where it lies to where it lay,
in desert dust, unfertilised, dormant now, no budding wise,
but then the outcast; suffered much, discovered seed to bend and touch,
wonders now; can it be . . . to give my mind and soul to thee?
So what's the catch and what's the cost? Renounce a world that I had
lost, descend to pit and furthermore, fight the demons; hellish war,
need it must, that I will go, to tranquil land of conquered woe,
when I deserve this heaven's bliss, saints and angels grant the wish,
that all the struggle, torment, strife, was not in vain; a means to life,
so I ascend toward the high, above the turgid, bid goodbye,
the answer's here as you well know, suffer mortal's bitter blow,
then you see what poet's meant, gratuitous, life misspent,
up to heaven; so I went, faith in justice: wonderment.

C Thornton

SONNET FOR THE MILLENNIUM

Show me a world where the watchword is peace,
Where love holds sway and hostilities cease,
And neighbourliness is more than a word
And cries for help go no longer unheard.
Show me a world where the birds and the bees,
The creatures of earth, the fish in the seas,
Can live and move in their own element,
Pollution forgotten, the pain long spent.

This is my dream, Lord, I hope it comes true,
Eden in England, the wider world too -
Tho' so much is wrong that setting it right
Would seem less likely than sunshine at night!
   Or me writing 'Once more unto the breach'
   Or a poem as good as Dover Beach.

Sheila Burnett

FULL CIRCLE

Come on, this won't do
Get up you must see the day through
Get dressed, have your breakfast, put on a smile
Take a deep breath, open the door, go out for a while.
Your situation may have altered but outside the world goes on
You've taken a fall this could happen to anyone.
Life's never fair, and never will be
At this moment it's difficult to see.

During the day much acting and yearning
Then at night much tossing and turning
And in the morning it all starts again
If only some one could take away the pain.

Gladys C'Ailceta

THE SONG OF SPACE

I move silently
upon the comet-littered
star path
passing the sun held planets
who are sleeping
in the black blanket
of the cosmic night . . .

I leave the solar system
and our familiar Milky Way
and journey to immense galaxies
whose creation and make up
are beyond the comprehension
of striving human minds
as they are totally unfamiliar to us

and then I heard
the deep throbbing
harmony of the universe
the song of space
a resonance which vibrated
my whole being
body, mind and spirit
transforming me to another dimension.

A new dimension
a new cosmos
an environment where evil
does not exist
here is a place of peace
where caring understanding
spreads happiness and kindness
as celestial wisdom
fills the cosmos with sacred hope . . .

Stephen Gyles

GEORGE AND I

I was only eighteen when I met my only love,
And peace came to us like a dove.
We met as cyclists on our way,
It was in the merry month of May.

He lived in Richmond and I in York,
So to meet two evenings a week, couldn't walk.
To Boroughbridge we cycled and stayed one hour,
This was all that was in our power.

We both raced, and rode our bikes for a hundred miles,
This was on Sundays, when we left each other there was sighs.
Three years later we got wed,
Down the aisle I was led.

This marriage lasted forty-four years,
It brought joy and also tears.
Thirty of this I was wheelchair bound,
So there was many tears.

One night in May he said 'It's sunny, can I go for a bike ride?'
I said 'You go, have a nice time,' but on the bike he died.
He had a massive coronary and died on the bike under an oak tree,
When I was told I felt God has taken him from me.

I knew it was a blessing and with God's help would cope,
Together we'd had happiness and love more than some folk.
I'm still grieving four years on,
But lovely memories keep coming along.

Pamela Earl

SIN POURED SCORN

Sin poured scorn when he knelt
There in Gethsamane
And when he hung their on Calvary

Sin poured scorn
When it mocked and ridiculed Him
And treated Him like a commoner
When it gave Him thorns for a crown
And bitter gall to drink

Sin poured scorn
When it drove the nails in His hands, feet and side
And mocked when its weight fell heavily on Him
And honoured a criminal more than Him

Sin poured scorn
And sold Him for thirty pieces of coins
And cast lots for His garment
It watched His every drop of blood
Spilled upon the ground
Between the two thieves

It rejoiced with Satan
When He cried to His Father

But alas
Sin was conquered
When He pronounced it is finished
I have conquered Satan is defeated.

Joyce A W Arnold

THE MIRACLE

Sweet Holy Spirit
I praise God for you
How you shed light and purpose
To carry us through
When your light is shed
Understanding is sweet
We wonder why so long
We have dragged our feet
And carried around resentment and fear
With no room at all for your help to appear
You were sent by God to this world
So that we
Could know him in all truth
And would be set free
Thank you for your light
Which has shown to me
That I can escape from the darkness in me
This is a miracle wrought by the Lord
Cause for the last nine years
Your grace was out poured
I had prayer upon prayer
To shift this Lord
But I could not make it roll
Down the road
Until I met Judy
Whom you had ordained
To be in my life to assist with this pain
Last week I knew a deep burden inside
No longer would this pain be denied
I wrote it all down and gave it to you
Not knowing precisely what you would do
I went through a time when there was a void
I knew my deep anger had been destroyed
But what's in its place?

Could this be right
There was nothing -
No absolutely nothing in sight
I know now Lord I was in-between
The place before peace
Where the grief had been
I was used to carrying
This heavy load
What would I do now
There was nothing to hold
Thank you dear Lord I now
Have it plain
You've given me joy
To replace all the pain

Claire Bloomfield

DARK AND SHADOW

There was shadow, on the hill,
not yet dark, what is come
of the night, expecting the stars
to shine. There is light in the
darkness and a little shadow
in the light of Christ, the holy
ghost, is come to brighten
the fleeting shadows journey
to the coast, where seas and
oceans meet, o' salt water, that
is near, in the night. Sunlight
brings with it, the warmth of
summer and the winter's dark and
cold, that shadow moves like wind
in the sails of ships out at
sea. I will make my journey, by
the stars, in the darkness of the
night, the shadow of a ship
appears with ghostly pallor, is
it shadow or ghost, the
white glimpse of sail out
of the ocean and the night, there
flits, remembrance like as I,
ghosts and tall ships about there fee,
what do shadows, confess
to all, the holy ghost has saved us
all and the light of Christ shines
in the darkness like
a ghost!

Robert Robb

WHY GO TO CHURCH?

'Why go to church?' a friend once asked,
'I'll attend a christening, a wedding, even a funeral,
But I draw the line at regular commitment.
Why, I've got better things to do with my time . . .
Football training, a swim,
a work-out at the gym.
Sunday is my only day for a lie-in,
to read the paper,
to drink a leisurely cup of coffee.'

'I don't have time to visit to my local church
or to think about God.
When I'm less busy I might consider Christianity . . .
maybe when I retire.'

'What a pity,' I thought,
'There must be thousands of people like you,
living only for themselves,
giving God the lowest priority in their lives.'

Cathy Mearman

KEEPER OF MY HEART

When the way is dark and drear . . .
And my heart begins to fear,
If I think that I might fall . . .
I have only to recall,
That, God is the keeper of my heart . . .

When my heart lays bleeding, sore and torn . . .
God shelters me from all the storm,
He watches over me night and day,
It is to Him alone, I pray.

Guardian Guide, and Shepherd is He . . .
Jesus who died upon the tree . . .
For, from the very start:
God, is the keeper of my heart . . .

Carol Olson

THE CHRIST

One who came to make know, a freedom to all the suffering of
mankind, an end was in sight.
Smiles on a face would be the way of life, no tears would be seen
to flow, the earth would flow with ways of peace.
No stains from the blood of life would the earth conceal from all
searching eyes,
Hearts rejoice with the beasts of the fields, no haven will visit anyone,
free at last to enjoy all the wonders of the Earth.
Now at this time we have a real need to have eyes of faith,
not doubting the truth of the ones that dwell alone,
the powers that gave us life at the very start, unlike man on Earth,
at this time, heaven's ways never change, the heavens have a day in
store, to set all mankind free from pain -of both the body and the mind.
Even the powers of death will never be see again,
shadows of death replaced by endless days of joy -
life will have full meaning to the very living soul, no one alive
will say they are sick, all will be forgiven for their former ways of life -
a world set free at long last to enjoy to the full creation's works of art -
all the seasons becoming as one season, leaves on trees will be seen
all year round.
They will blossom as a rose - our Earth will have returned
to ways belonging to an endless paradise.
Come Lord Jesus, come quickly.
Amen and amen.

R P Scannell

LORD... YOU!

Nonsense:
Simpletons, here!
A spiritual pretence!
False, worldly 'cheer' . . .
Offence?

Night-time
Over this side:
Hearts, delivered of crime
And earthly pride,
On time!

My Lord:
Your silence, here -
The perpetual cord:
Your gift of prayer . . .
Onward!

The best 'thing' . . . all day,
Was Thine immeasurable love
In our brother, the nurse, on the way,
Amidst the trial, and the shove . . .

Now, quiet remaining:
Thy still, night's grace -
The Holy Word, sustaining
My spirit . . . this place.

Tied, two
Remnants of verse . . .
Spirit of God's breakthrough,
Bringing such peace, as things got worse . . .
Tranquillity, in blue;
And, in the hearse,
Lord . . . You!

Richard D Reddell

REMEMBER

When you enter life's December,
Will you smile or fret?
What of life will you remember?
What will you regret?
When you face the final curtain,
Nearing your last breath,
When at last you know for certain,
You are near to death,
Were you harsh and unforgiving?
Living just for self,
Did you think that you were living,
Just for power or wealth?
Were you cruel, cold and grudging?
Were you kind and true?
Did you know who would judging,
What you chose to do?
Will the way that you've been living,
Fill your heart with dread?
Remember, you're beyond forgiving,
After you are dead.

Matthew L Burns

BE THANKFUL

There's lots to do on holiday,
Your days are really full,
Places to see, walks to go,
Or relaxing by the pool.

It's also a time you meet with folk,
And have a little chat,
Hear about their background,
Their town, their house or flat.

One day I met a lady,
She was completely on her own,
I felt her utter loneliness,
For she had cause to moan.

A year ago her hubby died,
It was hard for her to bear,
But as she said 'Life must go on,'
She just pretended he was there.

How brave she was to return again,
Do all the things they'd done,
But God had given her the strength,
Her sorrow she'd overcome.

So now when I'm inclined to moan,
Or say 'My life I hate,'
I'll think of her so all alone,
And feel blessed I have my mate.

Margaret Findlay

The Baby

The wee baby lay in a makeshift bed,
It was a manger in a cattle shed.
His sweet Mother Mary looked down with pride
On that tiny mortal by her side.

The shepherds came as the angel said,
They followed the star to the baby's bed,
And were amazed by the aura, in which he lay
So on their knees they knelt to pray.

Then came the three kings from afar
With gifts of gold and frankincense and myrrh.
They felt a presence they could not understand
So they knelt down together, a royal band.

The baby grew as babies do
And childish games he did pursue.
He was a child so fair, so good,
He was of course the Son of God.

Muriel Johnson

MARRIAGE BLESSING

On this great day deep vows are shared,
rings exchanged; sworn loving care -
at altar's kiss each soul laid bare;
two people become wedded pair.

Hearts can't contain the joy and pride
we, as parents, would not hide;
high and long and deep and wide
is love that you nurture inside.

We bless the moment that you met,
pray God gifts life free of fret -
and swear the children, unborn yet,
shall have our blessings too. You bet!

Perry McDaid

THE SHEPHERD ON THE HILLSIDE

The shepherd on the hillside
While tending his sheep
Tripped in a crevice and
Fell down the mountain steep.
As he rolled over and over
He wondered in his head
Whether he would stay alive
Or whether he was dead.
Landing on a rocky ledge
With no injury at all
He prayed to God to thank Him
For breaking his fall.
He sat there for a moment
Thinking how long ago
Shepherds working in the fields
Had feared the Angels so.
Yet without question
They left before dawn
To see a new baby
Which just had been born.
He wished he could have been there
To worship and sing
To see Mary and Joseph
And the gifts for the king.
But now he was thankful
And prayed once again
To thank God for Jesus
A King among men.

E M Gough

SACRIFICE

God gave us hope when there was none,
He sent to the world His beloved Son,
But how did we repay this loving act?
We nailed Him to a Cross with thorns for a hat,
His loving ways and gentle grace,
Were all thrown back into His face,
The things He did and the words He said,
Why did we all want Him dead?
We couldn't believe anyone could be so good,
How I wish that we had understood,
God sent His Son for us to love,
But we made Him go back to Heaven above,
We all realised what we had done far too late,
Now the world is paying for its fate.
We were given hope when there was none,
God knows that justice will be done.

Sandy Grebby

THY KINGDOM COME

Family bereft, incomplete
   Gone brothers mine
For what might have been
   Special moments lost, I sigh.

Family close, happy
   Sisters, Mum, Dad,
Sharing joys to be
   Troubles in times bad.

Farewell, dear brothers
   'Til my time comes
Forsake all others
   Life's journey done.

Life bitter-sweet to cling
   I ask God's love, grace.
Rest 'neath spread of angel wing
   In thy Kingdom's heavenly place.

Ivy Lott

THE BROTHERS

There once were thirteen brothers,
Who loved each other like no others,
One was hung from yonder tree,
For betraying the Father to a Pharisee,
The Father was tortured on a cross,
The brothers wept at the loss,
One brother denied the Father thrice,
As cock crowed in the morn,
The deed was done it was forsworn,
The other brothers were distraught,
All their hopes had come to naught,
One was a fisherman, for fish he caught,
The Father told him and taught,
To cast his net far and wide,
To where the souls of men abide,
And proclaim his words with pride,
And tell of the virgin bride,
And set the flame of gospel deep inside,
Let him come hither, let him not hide,
So now we have the Apostles' Creed,
Give up anger! Give up greed,
The brothers swore to help those in need.
It's up to you, if they succeed.

Alan Pow

A Lenten Offering

Christians wonder during Lent
what sacrifice to make
to help them truly to repent
for their Lord Jesus' sake.

Some give up their favourite thing
and hope from day to day
their efforts made in abstaining
atone for sins in some small way.

Of course the discipline is good
for the body, mind and soul;
We really must do all we should
and always strive to reach our goal.

But we can do so many things
in this blesséd time of Lent;
We can help the sick and suffering
and use our gifts that God has sent.

We cannot go to foreign lands
although we wish we could,
to maybe give a helping hand
and give the starving all we should.

But we can help in other ways
our wealth we can freely give
to try to lighten the sad days
of those who find it hard to live.

If we look around us now
and see what can be done,
let's pray that God will show us how
to do this work for His own Son.

Joyce Angel

My Guide

Lord Jesus is my faithful guide,
For me He's laid a track.
And when I wander far and wide,
Will always lead me back.

Now such a guide could be yours too,
If on *Him* you will call,
Always there to show the way,
And help in case you fall.

Now many others follow 'Him'
And I'm sure they all agree,
That 'Jesus' is the finest guide,
So try Him, is my plea.

I know that once you've made your choice,
You never will look back,
And with His daily help will find,
There is no better track.

So do not delay, just start today,
There is no better time,
The longer left, you will find,
Will be a harder climb.

Will A Tilyard

SUCH A LOVE AS THIS,
(A song for Easter)

What love is this
That He should die
For such people
Like you and I?

Such a love as this
The world should know
Just how much Jesus
Has loved them so.

His great love for me
I would never alter
Even though I fail
And sometimes falter.

Such a love as this
I can never fully,
Or really understand,
But I love Him truly.

My love is not like
His love for me,
As my love is weak
And not always free.

But I love Him truly
All of the same,
Because He died for me
And took all my blame.

John Harrold

MORE THAN I CAN BEAR...

To say I miss you's not enough!
How could it be when I'm in love?
I need to see you every day!
Can't stand it when you go away!
You board the plane! You skim the sky!
You cross the globe! You fly on high!
You leave me here, time on my hands...
Enough to pray that your plane lands!
Safe journey, loved one! Come back soon!
Your smiles to me are such a boon!
I miss you more as time goes on...
I pine for you while you are gone...
I ache inside each time you leave...
You'll never know how much I grieve...
At first I wept, I missed you so...
I never knew that love could grow!
Absence makes the heart grow fonder!
When you're back your hair is blonder!
Your eyes are bluer than the sky!
Your lips are redder! My, oh my!
Your curves seem curvier to me!
You truly are a sight to see!
Your smiles, of which I never tire,
Fulfil my soul, thus I admire
The miracle that I call you...
Such that no other girl will do!
I know God's blessed your destiny...
Though I miss you, do you miss me?
Do you pray that we'll reunite?
My darling, must you take that flight?

Denis Martindale

NEW COVENANT

'When you partake of this bread'
Our Saviour said,
'In its breaking remember me'
Jesus, a sacrifice of love,
Hung on a cross for thee.

'When you drink of this wine'
Our Saviour said,
'In its pouring remember me'
Jesus, a sacrifice of love,
His blood shed for thee.

But thought Our Lord died
He now lives again and in
Our Father's kingdom reigns,
He said 'I won't drink of this wine
Till I drink one that's new for
My blood seals God's
Covenant with you.'

Mazard (Micky) Hunter

WISHING ME BLUE SKIES

A branch, just outside my window,
Dips prettily;
Wishing me,
Blue skies,
And hearty laughter.

Bird bosom melody,
Chortly chirps,
Language of genuine feeling;
Is joy,
Beseeching futherance of favour.

A branch, dips, just so.
Birds, a song, for the morning.
Blue love voice, in sky;
The soul stirs,
And reaches out, to touch, and stay.

Rowland Warambwa

SANTA'S CHRISTMAS JOURNEY

Dear Santa with his reindeer fly
Across the starry night-lit sky
Bringing Christmas cheer to all
In answer to each urgent call
Gifts with messages filled with love
Fall like snowflakes from above
His task throughout the world is great
Protected by the heavenly gate
God is his guide across the blue
The stars his candles to see him through
Via Bethlehem's glowing brightest star
Its gift of light o'er the world afar
Give thanks to Santa and his team
Bringing the Christmas magic while we dream.

Ernest Hannam

GREATNESS

'Greatness' has no mantle of greatness
but a Mother's empty and barren womb
'Greatness' holds many plaudits and epitaphs
that can be worn on the adored Hercules,
'Greatness' is a reclusive master who,
taunts the individual at every step of his
seemingly glorious quest for life's rich and holy grails.

'Greatness' once started by our Genius
and noble gladiator, bathes in endless sunshine
that hides the thorn-riddled traps that await his victor's journey's end.

'Greatness' rewards in lavish praise and laurels of scented
trophies that adorn his hero in his lonely room.

'Greatness' then puts to rest (echoes of valiant past works done)
mocking at every turn.

'Greatness' tells no man, that the price one has to pay is paid
not in rich friendships and a family's love but 'tears' that could
fill the Nile were she empty.

'Greatness' (true happiness) and victory lies not in valiant
and heroic individual quests, but in the essence, the nucleus
of life itself.

The gift of life (God) is the only quest and journey that holds
recipient gains and victory.

'Greatness' is a shadowy and lonely Master who is barren and
beggared of soul and all who vaunt her ways are showered with
meaningless fool's gold.

'Greatness', the fool's friend, but life, love and friendship are the
'true' goals that reward in endless abundance for life's labours done.

John Gaze

MY PRAYER

Dear Lord, I thank you in every day:
For blessing me in every way.

May 'best of health' be given to all
Till we receive your final call.

C Shanks

MY THANKS

There are days in this work
When I feel all is lost
When tiredness prevails
Yet I don't count the cost
But I have in my life
Such a bright guiding light
That encases my being
By day and by night
I thank you, Dear Lord,
For your love and your care
And for giving me strength
When no strength is there
I thank you for being my rock and my guide
And pray I live always with *You* by my side.

Wendy Souter

TOUCHING HANDS

A Heavenly atmosphere
is made
When Hands touch Hands
and Love conveyed -
And Angels share in
Praise to God
For sending us
Our Saviour Lord.
Within the realms of
each New Age
He gives perfection
to appraise
'His Touch'
so tender
Leads us to
A school of Love we
never knew -
How wonderful the Prize
will be
When Hands touch Hands
across the Sea.

Mary Skelton

CALVARY

The seas do roar at the sound of your name
Yesterday, today, forever the same,
We change but you changeth not,
You without blemish, stain, or spot.

God saw the world lost and undone,
So He sent His beloved Son,
To die upon Calvary's tree,
From our sin to set us free.

The invitation He gives to all,
To all at His feet humbly fall,
Open your heart's door and let Him in,
And your heart will be washed free from sin.

Then you will know redemption story
And your name will be written down in glory
And your sins will forgiven be
All because of Calvary.

David Reynoldson

CHRISTMAS 2000

In late December days,
When sunset pushes teatime into darkness,
And tingling toes and fingers from without
Are warmed by inside, hearthside glow,
What else more can dark winter gloom us by?

The ice and snow? The wind and rain?
The too-low, soon-go, slow-glow sun?

But listen!
Hear the singing words which tell us of the Child.
The Man-Child.
The Man-Child King!
The Man-Child King of Kings
Who comes to us on Christmas morn!

So sing!

Frank L Appleyard

CHRISTIAN FRIENDSHIP

You are like a breath of fresh air
Sweet and kind, and you always care
Even when you are not always there
You provide encouragement and hope
in all the things that you share
and always remember me in a prayer

When I pray to God our Heavenly Father
I keep and continue to remember you
In my thoughts and in my prayers
Giving thanks to God for knowing you
As such a dear precious friend in Christ.

Gordon W Hendry

IN SPLENDOUR ABLAZE

In splendour ablaze
Are the rays of the sun
As dying its days
On earth it has run
In splendour ablaze
The rays of the moon
Through darkness at night
The morn comes too soon
In splendour ablaze
Is the song of the birds
Their voices they raise
Throughout all the earth
The earth's filled with splendour
The flowers and the trees
Each calling God's name
His imprint to please
In splendour ablaze
We each are to be
His image and likeness
For all men to see
Give God the glory
Give God the praise
Tell the world's story
In splendour ablaze.

Jean Turner

GETHSEMANE?

Come with Me to Galilee where
The fishermen were called
Gethsemane?
Witness My healing Hand
Marvel at the miracle of the raising
Of the dead *Gethsemane?*
Walk beside the donkey, children
Milling, waving palm leaves 'round
My head *Gethsemane?*

Come! And share a meal with Me
Let Me kneel and wash your feet
Drink the wine - the blood - I'll shed
My - body - broken - in - the - bread
Gethsemane?
Come to Gethsemane,
It is very different there!
Lonely, hurting, sweating blood,
Weighted already by the Cross
Will you still be there?
Gethsemane?

'Father, I will drink the Cup
According to your will'
Will you follow Me that far?
Will you be there still?
Gethsemane?

Cynthia Taylor

SOME MEN

Some men live in mansions
Where they hide their wealth away
From all the harsh realities
Life witnesses each day,
And some men live for nothing more
Than just a crust of bread
To see them through another day
Of burying their dead,
But a poor man's rich as a rich man's poor
When eternity opens up its door.

Some men take far more from life
Than a life's prepared to give
While there are famine-stricken lands
Where dying is to live,
And some men take away the pain
Of living on the street
By sharing their humanity
With all who face defeat,
But a poor man's rich as a rich man's poor
When eternity opens up its door.

Some men seek what they desire
Through mortal sin and such
But they are never satisfied
Or find the common touch,
And some men seek a better life
Through peace and harmony
Despite life's unrelenting wind
Of abject poverty,
But a poor man's rich as a rich man's poor
When eternity opens up its door.

Iaian W Wade

THE COMFORTER

Whatever changes life may bring
   I rest my all on God my King
A shelter from the storms that blow
   And trials that beset us so
In him I trust who doth me lead
   A bulwark in the hour of need.

Should I encounter foes around
   Set thou my feet on firmer ground
Content that in your love and care
   I am secure in all I share
And in your presence I shall find
   Assurance and a carefree mind.

R T James

LIFE IS A STORYBOOK

My life is like a storybook
It starts off with the cover.
You have to have a title or name
The authors being your father and mother.
Then the book is opened, introduction your beginning.
As pages and chapters unfold, it can become very intriguing.
You don't know what is coming next it reads as life goes on
Then you go back on yourself because the storyline is gone.
You suddenly come to the swings and roundabouts that can
                                                            be very exciting
Then the never-ending rollercoaster that brings horror
                                                            unreal and beguiling.
Sometimes the sun does shine, bringing with it all its glory
It brings romance and happiness to boost up your life's story.
Then you reach middle age, being the centrefold of your book.
You come to many cross-roads but don't turn back to take a look.
You need a break and a pause, you end another chapter and the
                                                            book you close
Feeling refreshed you then pick up the book to start another chapter
Hoping by now it will bring you fun and plenty of humour and laughter.
The pages turn like every day and chapters pass so quickly
Excitement builds up as the final chapter approaches very swiftly.
Your destination is at hand hoping for a happy ending
But that is something I don't know and it makes it all mind-bending.
So for now I'll close my book and put it safely on the shelf
As by now you must realise I cannot finish it myself.
So my conclusion up to now is very unpredictable
And hope that my life's story does not turn out to be predictable.

Irene Smith

WHAT BE THE POINT?

What be the point of life
Without you in it?
There is no laughter without your smile
What be the point of breath
Without your name upon it?
What be the point of life?
There is no need for eyes
Without seeing you in them
There is no laughter without your smile
What be the point of arms
Without holding you in them?
What be the point of life?
There is no night to sleep in
Without you to lie beside
There is no laughter without your smile
What be the point of the moon in the sky
Without your love as its guide?
What be the point of life?
There is no laughter without your smile.

L J Doel

ENDURANCE

Dear Loving God we trust and pray
That Christian martyrs of today
Will find your strength in times of pain -
When courage can begin to wane.

May they feel you very near
And focus on their Saviour dear.
May they remember - on a cross
Jesus too felt at a loss.
'My God, My God, why have you forsaken me?'
Crying out again - did He.

Dear Loving God again we pray
That they'll remember every day
God is with them though unseen
And the path they tread is where You've been.

O God - for martyrs everywhere
We offer thoughts in humble prayer
And thank You that they'll never lose
Their precious soul - *This is good news!*

Amen

Pat Melbourn

BURNING TRAILS

Tracing your fiery footsteps
Understanding what you went through,
Those fires you kindled
Were never meant to destroy you.
Trail-blazing is never easy
Laying it all on the line,
Exploding pressures engulfed you
Drove you out of your mind.

Burning candles at both ends
Spending hours all alone,
Pushing yourself on
Even unhooking the phone.
Hot words erupted
Lids came off,
Struggling for perfection
Nothing ever good enough.

Saw the fire in your eyes
Flames shooting from your heart,
Mind-searing dreams
That would not depart.
Those burning trails you followed
Others feared to tread,
Tried to teach them the way,
They would not be led.

Remembering those burning trails
Passing this way again
Picking up the fragments
Dedicating them to your name.

Ian Barton

SPIRITUAL SEEDS
(Dedicated to Kev Doran)

As if we were split from the same seed
Someone on whom I can always depend.

Who cares not for what we've got
Knowing we'd always share our little lot.

A listening ear to lend or bend.

In my darkest hours he's always there
Giving me reassuring words of comfort and care.

He understands my vulnerable side
Shared in my pain and tears I've cried.

In a world blinded by materialistic greed
Still we nurture each other's spiritual needs.

Nothing crushes our friendship's seeds.

Sometimes we all feel sad and blue
That's when a special friend
Can pull you through.

I thank God I am blessed
To have a friend like you.

Graham Hare

MARY
(Blessed art thou among women)

Mary, a sad lonely figure
at the foot of the cross.

****

Imagine Mary's deep
agonising sorrow as
Jesus spoke to her from
the cross.
With shock she would
be numb, stunned and
her mind at a loss.
But her heart cried out
'What have they done to
you, my Son of God?
You came to bring peace
love and light.
This has been your life's
ambition, to care for the
sick, lonely and lost.
And this is the cost.
The fault of jealous,
frightened men, who twisted
your words and deeds
until seeds of evil festered
and erupted.
What have they done to you
my Son of God?'

Mary, mothers the world over
bow their heads in sorrow

We know Mary you would
never stop loving God
your Creator, for after all,
this madness was
created by man himself.
he did God and himself
a great injustice.

Elizabeth Myra Crellin

REVELATION

Revelation is a wonderful thing,
It opens closed minds and lets you peep in.
Past, future and present become crystal-clear.
It takes away uncertainty and
Allows you to act without failure or fear.
Revelation shines a hopeful light
Upon dread, darkness and helpless tears.
The gloom and doom is at once lifted and a way forward appears.
Take comfort and believe there is always
Hope, faith and prayer on the wing.
Open your heart, trust and believe,
Angel's guidance will help you through everything.

Amelia Michael

LOVE'S FIRST DECREE

Those scribes before men's eyes now wish to show
Light fashion intellectual pages.
They produce a dance of death, the wages
For John the Baptist, the saint taken low.
Then Herod dismembered the live glow
Of children's limbs and lives in short stages.
Those children created the smile within cages
Upon the lips of emptiness that crow.
Then Heaven's great originality
Of goodness walks within to set them free.
They do all see the power, the glory
Of Christ the Lord and feel love's first decree.
The death hills are made of loneliness
God rejects this forever then does bless.

Edmund Saint George Mooney

MY REALLY GOOD FRIEND

I like to think there's a God somewhere,
great big Dad to the human race;
it seems that He really does care -
I guess there's concern on His face,
but then He's not a person like
the guys, my father and my mum,
He drives no car nor rides a bike,
just gathers prayers as fast as they come,
a spirit like a friendly ghost,
magic and mystical, divine;
from what I'm told He is the most
devoted friend of all of mine.
I'm just an ordinary boy
with faults upon a frightful scale
but God exists and there is joy
in doing good, though I bewail
separation from computer
to do the things I'm asked to do
yet I know there's a mighty Tutor
beyond the skies of azure hue,
misted sometimes by rain and cloud,
a fine example to uphold;
I wonder if I'll make Him proud
of me by the time I'm old.
Some little 'tearaways' despair
of Him and do disgraceful crime.
I feel it really isn't fair,
doing wrong with Him there all the time.

Ruth Daviat

UNTITLED

Early morning, silence reigns upon the empty streets,
Suddenly, the echo of my footsteps tracing the familiar route to Sunday worship,
Invade the tranquillity that exists.
I smell the dampness and feel the touch of the cold morning air upon my skin,
Conscious that my presence feels alien in this naturally sedate world.

My mind in turmoil,
Full of inconsequential thoughts carried over from the busy week prior, contrasts with the peaceful atmosphere.
The warm touch of the sun's rays penetrate my thoughts,
I am awakened to the present moment.
My eyes are opened to the beauty that surrounds me in these quiet urban streets that only yesterday seemed so ugly.

I see the early morning dew glistening like tiny jewels on the individual blades of grass; the small green shoots of spring's first bulbs piercing the grass verges once strewn with litter; the contrasting shade of green from the trees and bushes outlining the distant horizon, highlighted by the sun's reflective rays as it emerges from behind the clouds.

The sound of birds suddenly breaking into song interrupt my peaceful vision and alert me to the fact that no longer do I feel alien in this wonderful work of creation,
But truly belong.
My soul has been touched by God's hand.

Janice Frazer

I Long To Be...

Where the sky is so blue
Dreams do come true
Happiness reigns, in a world free of pain
Crystal-clear waters, run down to the sea
That is the place, I long to be.

Fields of flowers, are kissed by the showers
Children play games, fall in love without shame
The moon shines so bright, on a star-studded night
Family and friends are all there with me
That is the place I long to be.

Song birds all sing, people have everything
No malice or shame, life's just a game
People roam free, beautiful sights there to see
That is the place, I long to be.

There is no violence, or war,
No one has secrets, no one is poor
Faith has a meaning. Respect one another
People are equal, he is your brother
Prayers are all answered, it's so good to be
There in that place, I long to be . . .

GIG

Lost And Found

I can't return to childhood's praise
For nature's beauties. Since that dawn
I've come to know the darker side.
A silent song is now aroused
By novel facts unearthed by hard
And costly toil. The starker hues
Of rampant strife, the secret role
Of parasites, the dastard toll
From viruses in league with death,
All these are truths I can't deny.
And yet these constant wars bequeath
Us life in all its rich array
Of diverse forms and modes. With awe
I learned of wonders man can scarce
Conceive. Resourceful tricks, and slick
Solutions shaped from bum designs
Selection had no choice but hone,
I find abound. So now I feel
Profound respect, in place of thanks
I gave as child. I still perceive
Delight is right, but worship's praise
Is now reserved for God alone.
His grace accepts us as we are,
But summons us to rise above
The selfish beasts from which we've come.
We're called to walk the way of love
That renders death a passing phase,
That gives us hope beyond the grave.

Henry Disney

THE SOLITARY MAN

God works in mysterious ways,
how true that seems to be,
it's hard to understand why
he chooses people to die.
Death is so final it breaks the bond of life
my brother is in mourning for his beloved wife.
So as he comes to terms with being on his own
in my prayers I ask for peace of mind
and strength for him alone.
No words of comfort can be said
the grief and shock's too deep,
he sits and silently stares into space
a look of disbelief upon his face.
He is going through the motions
of cleaning, eating, drinking,
but nobody on this earth
knows what the poor man's thinking.
They say time heals and pains subside
at the moment that's hard to believe
but God I'm sure will guide him
and will tend to his every need.

Linda Beavis

THE BEST

Something us women ne'er allowed to forget,
Babies do not pop out like a cork!
A good bit of shoving is needed,
Pain is part of the score,
But oh! What delight we drool on the bairn,
Mess, trouble, tears, soon forgotten.

Women meet up with worry galore,
Getting a mate, setting up house,
Working, cleaning, rearing,
Keeping the whole scenario going,
Carrying the burden no matter the package,
Funny most have a saying, 'We'll manage'.

Then those mystery beings with flair,
Ask them to jump a ditch, what a stir!
They only see mud in the middle,
Wee consultation, think tank turned on,
Such was the plight of the weeping disciples,
Not foresighted women with aloe and myrrh.

Jesus, God in flesh, advent a manger,
Mary's forethought in love swaddling clothes,
Same love spurred women to anoint His dead body,
Stone already rolled away, God's honour to them,
Who, He our risen Saviour first appeared to?
Mary of Magdala, out of whom He had seven demons cast.

Ancient Eve set our World on its travels,
On knowledge's road we since then have struggled,
Memory's lane tells an amazing tale,
Every Age, a woman to the occasion rose,
God's laugh at the Devil (poor bugger),
'People let Me down, I only raise them up!' God.

Anne Mary McMullan

I Wanted...

I wanted to build a temple for you.
I wanted to build the house of God.
I wanted the righteous pride that came with it.
I wanted to use my riches as best I could.
I wanted to show that I was so grateful
For all of the dangers that you led me through,
For that great moment when you had me anointed.
I wanted to show I'd not forgotten you.

I wanted to write a show that praised you.
I wanted to tell that you came to save.
I wanted the glory to all go to you Lord.
I wanted this play to go out in your name.
I wanted to show that I was so grateful
For saving my life when I was a small boy.
For giving me talent to write songs in abundance,
For taking my sin, making it null and void.

But the task was given to someone greater
- The man you endowed with a most wise insight,
A broad understanding that could not be measured,
Like sand on the seashore, like stars in the night.
I was not worthy (a past sin of fleshdom).
Only the holiest could be God's one choice;
And in the end, with the temple constructed
You know he listens to God's awesome voice.

Andrew Sanders

Laughter

When you are feeling poorly and low,
Your body is aching, you feel sluggish and slow;
Think something funny and get yourself laughing,
Then in a short while you'll feel like prancing.

You go to the doctor because you feel ill,
He gives you prescriptions for bottles of pills;
Take three times a day, says the label that's on it,
When most of the time, laughter's the best tonic.

The weather is bad, it makes you depressed,
You think you may as well stay in bed and rest;
Invite round some friends, have a laugh and a joke,
By the end of the day you'll throw off that yoke.

Don't let your troubles start getting you down,
Some people are worse off, so don't wear a frown;
Laugh and the world laughs with you, the saying goes,
Cry and you cry alone, this everyone knows.

So when you wake up each morning to start your day,
Stay quiet for a while and this you should pray;
'Dear Lord above, what this day has in store,
Help me face it with laughter, and not be a bore.'

Reg Cook

GOD'S LOVE

God will love you all the while,
You can face your troubles with a great big smile;
He's always with you every day,
Give Him your love and you'll find the way.

With God to love you all the time,
Your life on Earth will be sublime;
Love everyone as you travel life's path,
You'll find life is fun and always a laugh.

He is your shield wherever you are,
If you go for a walk or a drive in the car;
He will protect you where'er you may be,
God's love is there for you and for me.

Thelma Cook

THE SABBATH

Last day of the week,
I must sleep.
O, long boring day,
oblivion I seek.

Last day of the week,
must go to the shops.
When I return
I will get out the mops.

Last day of the week,
I am at home.
Must call the man
to mend the phone.

Too bad if he
makes a noise.
Must chase my own goals,
I have no choice.

But, the *first* day of the week
is the Sabbath Day,
given by God
to rest and pray.

The Sabbath Day
spent with God
is life for body and soul
recreating man whole.

O, blissful day!
Stop!
Walk
with the Lord as your stay.

Elaine McCulloch Smith

WHERE ARE YOU GOD?

From the troubles beset by the human race
God is constantly asked why He hides His face?
And why they are left to suffer alone
While God sits aloof ignoring each moan?

They ask in prayer, they plead in vain
For God to release them from their pain
God made them and they have been taught
In prayers to give God a thought

And to pray to Him when they are in need
If they were in trouble He would give heed
I am sure, though, that your prayer plays a part
And God hears and sends hope to your heart

So you don't sink too low in your mind
And from somewhere more courage you find
To make you reach out and help yourself
And from that point rise to a higher self

Then you will know it was not in vain
The prayer that you sent whilst in pain
The power that you found deep within
Made you come to a new beginning.

Roystone Herbert

SILENCE OF THE LAMBS

It's a joyful sight in spring to behold
The new-born lambs brought into the fold,
The tenderness of a mother's care,
The dependent trust so evident there.

Then tragedy strikes, dreaded foot and mouth,
And devastation from North to South,
Must drastic action now be taken,
Innocent animals suddenly forsaken?

Carcasses piled up in a funeral pyre,
Condemn the disease in a trial by fire,
On the poor farmers it takes its toll,
They're sad at heart, and sick in soul.

Does it have to be this - is there no other way
To keep this dreaded scourge at bay?
Only time will tell, when the slaughter's done,
What a costly price for the battle won,
... The Silence of the Lambs ...

All we like sheep had gone astray,
We'd turned every one to his own way,
But our Saviour Jesus - God's own Son,
Gave Himself for the battle o'er sin to be won.

The Lamb of God to slaughter was led,
But the grave couldn't hold Him - He rose from the dead!
Ascended now - with the Father in Glory,
A triumphant end - what a wonderful story!
... *Behold the Lamb of God, who takes away the sin of the World ... (John 1 v 29).*

Brian Fisher

To Give Of Peace

To give of peace, of quietness,
True Christian hearts will court despair
To search within the brokenness.

In city street, in faithfulness
Unending, love will find them there,
To give of peace, of quietness.

This love of God, which they confess,
Will take the sinner in, to care,
To search, within the brokenness.

Salvation's soldiers savour stress,
Fighting the fight, they win, who dare
To give of peace, of quietness.

And hardened heart they love no less
(Asleep in doorway, ruined, bare)
To search, within the brokenness.

Yet, in this shambles, in this mess,
They still find time to 'stand and stare',
To give of peace, of quietness,
To search within, the brokenness.

Roger Mosedale

TAKE AN INTEREST

We rub shoulders with many people as we go about our daily life.
It isn't possible to take an interest in everyone whom we meet
As some we meet just in passing.

But there may be some who are known to us,
Who may be in need.
Perhaps they don't have visitors,
And a kind word from us would help.
We could take an interest in them.

Could we fill that loneliness for them?
Could we fill that gap?
We may be doing a wonderful service
Which the heavenly Father will not fail to notice.
Everyone will be greatly blessed
And it will not be for any earthly reward
That these blessings are bestowed.

Maybe we need to take an interest in God's wonderful creation,
Flowers, with their colours of every hue.
Creatures of all kinds
The mountains, valleys, streams and lakes.
I am sure that God in Heaven, the Grand Creator of all
Will be greatly pleased by our interest in His handiwork.

God and His Son, Jesus, wrote their teachings in that grand book,
                                                    The Bible.
For they were there for us to take an interest,
Obedience to them will gain us eternal life
In a re-created earth, a wonderful paradise,
Life for all in perfection for evermore.

Thanks to the Heavenly Father and Saviour Jesus.
For setting us an example to follow.
In taking a real interest in all aspects of our life.

N Mason

GOD'S LOVE REACHES OUT

Dear God reach out to all who need you
Out there in our troubled world
Seek hearts and minds
And encompass with your love
Guide the war-torn countries
Show your love to all
Who suffer every day
From weapons built by man
Which are used to kill and maim
Help children who are orphaned
Daily give them hope
Of a future free of fear
Show a way to peace, God
Let there be an end to war.

Watch over all who are disabled
Help the sick of body and in mind
Help all who suffer daily pain
Show compassion for the poor and needy
God, when a person is bereaved
They need you by their side
To give them strength to carry on
God, guide all who are in power
Help them through their troubled times

God make your presence felt
To all who go astray
Lead them to your door
The world that you created
Is very wonderful and precious
And with your daily guidance
It will always be that way.

Amen

Pamela D Jewell

TEACHING AND PREACHING THE WORD

The preacher teaches
of the Greatest Event
In the evolution of Man and the World.
The teacher preaches
Of the Laws of the Earth.
Both are adjacent, complementary flags unfurled
For the purpose of enlightenment
And the renewal of birth.
The Event of Palestine,
The Mystery of Golgotha,
Made Jesus yours and mine.
But do we really bother?
We place our faith
In material welfare.
We worship Mammon, not God!
We think all is external, in what lies without.
We think not of the Internal,
Where Eternal Truth allows no doubt.

Let us intensify Feeling,
And Thinking and the Will
To believe that the Healing
Of Body, Spirit and Soul
Comes from the Master within
The Destroyer of Ignorance, Sickness and Sin.

David Hill

JESUS, THE PEARL OF GREAT PRICE

Jesus, You are so dear,
    To my heart, be ever so near.
I love You Lord, You are the one,
    You are God's only beloved Son.

You suffered on the cross,
    Your mother must have felt the loss,
Also friend John and Mary too,
    Your friends forever true.

You rose from the grave,
    Sinners You want to save.
We are waiting for Your return,
    Your salvation we cannot earn.

Only by grace are we saved by You,
    We come to the Father through You.
Jesus is the Way, the Truth and the Life,
    We have to follow the path through strife.

We are better people through suffering and pain,
    In our hearts Jesus must reign.
Thank You Lord for being with me,
    Through life Jesus holds the key.

Thank you Lord,
    For Your saving grace.
I wish I could see,
    Your smiling face.

Elizabeth De Meza

THE FIRST MIRACLE

At the end of a season of sun and rain
The vines in the vineyard are laden
With fruit in its fullness - soon to be wine,
The finest in all the region;
But the natural cycle, year on year,
And the vine-grower's care and patience
Take months to do what Jesus did
The day of the wedding in Cana.

Sheila Burnett

SUFFER THE LITTLE CHILDREN

The world turns,
tyranny rules.
Oppressed people
living in squalor.
Rags and dirt!
Rags and dirt!

Greed abounds.
No one cares,
secure in their
own little world.
Profit and self!
Profit and self!

Food in silos stored,
waiting for the price
to rise.
A price the starving
cannot pay.
Taxes and Death!
Taxes and Death!

Dirty rags adorn
their backs,
dirty hovels to lay
their heads.
Meat and wine for
the Politician.
Hunger and thirst!
Hunger and thirst!

Politicians talk
and talk and talk,
care only for themselves
not for them the
cries and tears.

Self and greed!
Self and greed!
Why? The world
screams! Why?
The eternal question,
no one knows,
no one cares,

The world turns!
The world turns!

Sandy Chambers

WE ARE GOD'S CHILDREN

We have it all
Each day is a gift
Feel the love
Bringing boldness and joy

Come to His table
Take the bread
Share your life with Jesus
Praise the Lord

Love is overflowing
You can help the world
To be a better place.

Kenneth Mood

LET THIS BE

Let this be the day He promised
Graced by warmth and skies of blue
Where His peace flows like a river
Every moment all day through
Let this day bring nought but sunlight
Beaming freely from above
Constantly as breezes whisper
God is here and God is love.
Let this be the day He promised
When indeed we may suppose
He portrays His power and glory
In the beauty of a rose.
Look around and view His splendour
Etched upon each perfect flower
Ponder not why joyful songbird
Bursts with praise upon this hour
Let this be the day He promised
For no other can compare
Gaze in awe and you shall see Him
Caught in wonder everywhere.

Juliet Eaton

WHY?

He came to learn
To seek
To find
To encompass all in his mind
Because he knew
The mind and the soul are one
And the key to the mind is knowledge
To better your soul
And the gift is to impart this truth
So others find it too
And so the cycle goes on
Benefiting mankind.

Mary Shovlin

HE IS . . .

He is the root cause
  it's not the songs we sing
    or the word that pastors bring

      He is the root cause

        the world shall know and see
          if anything happens then it's because He
         is the root cause.

Francis McFaul

TAKING GOD FOR GRANTED

I sit and dream and wonder why
We take for granted our beautiful sky
I sit in awe at the setting sun
The morning light when each day's begun
At each new dawn as the birds do sing
I sit and muse what the day will bring
As flowers push forth in our magic earth
And all rejoice at each new birth
I wonder does God get mad at us
With trivial things we make a fuss
Does His patience ever wear thin?
When we can't be bothered to thank Him
For all the wonders He does bestow
He must get mad and want to show
How ungrateful we all can be
His eternal presence we just don't see
His gifts of flowers again and again
He waters them with His precious rain
He must feel mad, groan with despair
When we ask ourselves 'is He really there?'
When in dire straits it's 'Please help me God'
When lives run smooth, He is forgot
He must get lonely, He must feel sad
When we all forget Him, good and bad
It wouldn't take much to show we care
And end each day with a 'thank you' prayer.

Marlene Devlin

LOVE FROM WITHIN

To sift
Out the answers
In a World
So crazy
Is there any Truth
In the Reality you see
Or are you blind
To it all?
My Reality is different,
It's one of love
And definition
Of shape
And size
Sometimes indefinable.
Don't conquer love
With your hate
Look outside yourself
And you'll find
What's within.

Ruth Holder

EASTER

The crown of thorns is covered in blood
He hadn't deserved it.
What wrong had He done?
Only tried to spread His Father's word.
There had been some who listened,
There were some who believed.
Were they also tortured, suffering too?
Were they also regretting listening, and following too.
Oh Father! Dear Father! Spare their pain do!
Your love is so great, it encompasses us all
We are here to do your will, not to go to the wall.
The sun is now rising, a new day is born,
Rejoice up in Heaven for I will be there
Please listen, rejoicing, please hear my prayer.

P Wright

THE VALLEY WALK

I am walking unwillingly
Through the valley of the shadow of death
I drag my feet
It is a deep valley
Sunken to despair
No one wants to join me there
And tho' the others may walk the hilltops
Bathed in the golden sun
I am walking in the shadows
Where the light shines dimly
And all hope is diminished.

But wait,
    Did He not agree to meet me
    He promised at the end,
        to greet me
    With open arms
        and a warm welcome

But no,
    He promised more than that
    He promised He would walk with me
    On this sorrowful journey
    He said he would be
    A comfort and my company
    And tho' terrors in the shadows hide
    He would never ever leave me

As I walk through the valley of the shadow
                          of death.

S K Clark

IN YOUR STRUGGLE

He taught us diligently
We talked of them
While we sat in our house
While we walked by the way
And while we lay down
And when we rose up
Children! Obey your parents
In the Lord; for this is right
Honour your father and mother
That it may be well with you
And that you may live long on Earth
And you fathers, provoke not
Your children to wrath
But bring them up in the nurture
And admonition of the Lord
I have no greater joy
Than to hear that
My children walk in truth.

Ebenezer Essuman

WALK TO WONDERLAND

Our lives had been filled with much trouble and pain,
Each day was like walking out in the rain,
We tried to love as much as we could,
Then one day you took me for a walk in the wood.

We walked through the trees, it was spring you could tell,
Then you bent down and picked a lone bluebell,
Pulling me close you put the flower in my hair,
Giving a feeling of magic only you can share.

We drifted along holding each other by the hand,
The trees slowly parted showing us a magic land,
A carpet of bluebells surrounded by trees,
The beauty before us brought us to our knees.

We clung to each other lost in the beauty of this place,
I turned and looked at you, tears falling down my face,
You held me closer and the birds began to sing,
Then you whispered in my ear, please wear my gold ring.

Lesley Allen

LET YOUR SOUL BE FREE

Let your soul be free
Free like an eagle flying in the wind
Let your soul take in
Like a sponge that you found out of the sea.

Let your spirit sing
Sing high above the trees
Spread your wings and you shall see
That your soul opens up
And your spirit takes it in.

Angela Hovell

THOUGH

Though the hearts of all men, breaking,
Feel the strains of life's lament,
God will love and mend them, making
Life a joy, and hearts content;
Though we've lost our way through blindness,
To a world where love can rule,
God can lay the path to kindness
Using goodness as His tool:

Though the minds of men seek pleasure
Borne of status, greed and wealth;
God gives peace and life to treasure,
And the gift of lifelong health;
Though we worship at the altar
Money and its whims maintain;
Only God's great love won't falter
When we're faced with grief and pain.

Though in souls of men, lie lurking
Seeds of future woes and fear,
God, whose love is always working
Stays around, forever near:
Though some choose to shun, and doubt Him,
Faithless in their time on Earth;
None of us can live without Him
If we want to prove our worth.

Nicholas Winn

GRADUALLY AND GRATEFULLY

Many 'Billions of Years Ago', so I was told,
It was very Dark and Icy Cold.
In this 'Atmosphere', various crystals, began to form,
Eventually a Colossal Mass of Rock, was formed.
It became unbalanced, and began to spin,
This created, internal combustion, to begin.
When at Centrifugal Speed, it did go,
It exploded to form, the Galaxy, we now know.
Now there was Light, the Combustion, became our Sun,
And magnetic rotation of these new Planets had begun.
One piece of Rock, we call Earth, was now affected, by that Sun.
It's Icy covering, melted to become a sea,
Earth's internal combustion, made eruptions, to create land,
This would be our beginning, nature had planned.
From this new 'Environment', various Funguses began to grow,
As these fungus would cross-breed, to become grass and trees,
Fish would now develop, as some spores blew into the sea.
What once was blown around as fungus seed,
Evolution of life on Earth, developed rapidly.
I believe, this World's creations and creatures, today we see,
Could well be the beginning of You and Me . . .

Brian Marshall

GOD BLESSED US

God blessed the world,
With flowers and trees.
So we should look after it,
For it's Him we should please!

So have faith in the Lord,
Learn to share, no need for greed.
For he is with us all the time,
Not just in those times of need!

Show respect for new life,
And the fruits it doth bring,
Then we can give thanks,
Through the hymns that we sing!

Ann Beard

THE WEATHER:

Rain again - when will it ever stop?
And how hard the wind doth blow?
The rain wets everything in sight, drenching
Everyone from head to toe.
Nothing can be done about it
- Put up with it as best you can -
There must be something good come from it
- There must be something in God's plan!
But what this is we are not aware
And continue to moan and groan.
Rain again - it's never ending,
It's so very long since the sun shone.
The one essential piece of clothing
Which everyone needs this day,
Is a heavy duty rainproof
As we go along our way.
Let's hope before long there'll be a breakthrough
With a little of God's good grace.
And some sunshine will then come upon us
As we awake to see God's face.

Jean C Pease

The Sage

The sage, when young, his head maximises,
but, when old 'n wise, his heart optimises.
He distinguished himself by learning all his life,
and makes a discovery not just to survive.
Contemned or condemned, he eas'ly defeats morons;
prosecut' or executed, he beats mammons.

However, when'ver his work comes to light,
pseuds and frauds, hark! claim it their copyright,
leaving him penniless and oh! no happiness.
His enemies, victimisers and nemeses
are idlers and wiseacres, toadies 'n impostors,
otherwise called his inevitable tormentors.

Since Messiahs as well as prophets are poor,
he too life of poverty can endure,
knowing his way is ethics not economics.
Knavery and skulduggery are histrionics,
he muses, the stuff of infamy and calumny,
which then beget ignominy and tyranny.

Those, who sell their souls only for a song,
are corrupt, whose victory doesn't last long.
They live the momentary but he eternity,
life of dignity, admired by posterity.
Such greats are legion, like Plato and Socrates,
if not enough, also Bruno and Cervantes.

Rangram Boontarig

SPRINGTIME

When I woke up this morning and gazed around the room
It somehow seemed quite different, no more an enclosed tomb
I wondered why I felt so good, without a single care
And realised without a doubt that,
Spring was in the air.

I looked out of my window, saw the sun up in the sky
The bulbs out in the garden, I swear looked one inch high
I knew I must get out and walk, a thing with me most rare
It was good to feel, so young again
Cause spring was in the air.

So up the road, we went at last my little dog and me
Past gardens springing to life once more, some snowdrops I can see
Buds on the trees, birds on the nest - a fox lazed in his lair
The lambs were skipping round the field
Now spring was in the air.

I didn't notice time that day, as on my walk I went
Then suddenly the sun went in, and I felt really spent
My feet were sore, twas getting late, and time I turned around
So back I trudged, at peace with life, contentment I had found
Too soon like life the days would pass, and everything turn bare
So make the most of what you have
Whilst spring is in the air.

Mary Hayman

Maranatha! (Come Lord Jesus!)
(To be sung to the tune of 'Jesus Christ Is Risen Today)

If Jesus Christ were here today,	Maranatha!
Would He teach us how to pray?	Maranatha!
How to walk and talk with him?	Maranatha!
How to sing the second hymn?	Maranatha!
If Jesus Christ were here this morn?	Maranatha!
Would he watch us mow the lawn?	Maranatha!
Or sit upon our garden seat?	Maranatha!
He makes our flowers grow a treat!	Maranatha!
If Jesus Christ were here tonight?	Maranatha!
I think we'd almost die with fright!	Maranatha!
But perhaps we'd make Him Clipper tea!	Maranatha!
Or - if preferred -Traidcraft coffee!	Maranatha!
When Jesus Christ rides again,	Maranatha!
Will it be in the Virgin Train?	Maranatha!
Or riding on an old black bike?	Maranatha!
Or running - courtesy of Nike?	Maranatha!
Come Lord Jesus, come again!	Maranatha!
In the Word and in the wine!	Maranatha!
In Eucharist and daily strife,	Maranatha!
Hear our prayers and give us life!	Maranatha!
Come Lord Jesus, come to us!	Maranatha!
In your glory, on the bus!	Maranatha!
Sit by me and take my hand,	Maranatha!
And then I'll know that you're my friend.	Maranatha!

Reverend Eddy Burfitt

UNTITLED

How many words in the Bible are true?
And does it ever really affect you?
Psalms and gospels, hymns and praise
Arms and hostiles, men and graves.

Philip Allen

PEACE BE WITH YOU

(Julian of Norwich (c1342-1420) was an anchoress who lived in a little room attached to St Julian Church, referred to as her Cell. She was greatly respected by people who came to the window of her cell for counsel and prayer, and was the first English woman to have a book printed. In the Anglican lectionary she is commemorated on 8th May)

There is peace in Julian's cell,
Pilgrims know it well;
In the silence feel her presence,
Hear 'All shall be well'.

Norfolk's rivers flow
Not heeding care or woe.
Take time out to linger by one
And its peace you'll know.

The sun sets over Lynn
And homeward journeys now begin
Leave the planning, work and worry,
Rest, know peace within.

'Peace I leave with you' said the Lord.
On us all that gift was poured
Beyond earth's understand,
Whate'er our path afford.

For inner peace we thank you, Lord.

Jean Dorrington

WHOSE HAND ON THE TILLER?

She left in the dim light of dawn
A strange, sad day; nothing to say.
Just the closing of the door, forlorn
And bitter, as she picks up her bag
And hurriedly goes her way.

Tempers were lost the night before,
No feeble tongue, no joy or fears.
She weeps until she weeps no more,
Then calmly crosses the bedroom floor,
Head held high, wiping her tears.

I search by day and dream at night.
I dream that all will reveal
Whose hand is on the tiller,
Whose hand on the wheel.
Dear Lord let me see the light.

Where is my love, Oh where is she?
Many a face has passed me by.
I know them not!
They know not me!
Oh where, Oh where can she be?

The sun lies low in the sky.
I still wonder and wonder why
I have not prayed to my Maker before.
Is He not the anchor man
In this game of love and war?

On a bench seat by the wall,
Weary legs rest on aching frame.
I hear her voice, a gentle call.
I feel her presence by my side
And in her eyes I see the pain.

I hold her close will not let her go
And touch her face as hot tears flow.
Had I been blinded by brazen vanity,
Suspicion or savage jealousy?
Why, oh why! I do not know.

The glowing sun has set its course,
Drowning dark shadows with compelling force.
With yellow, greens and bright reds glowing,
Bright the canvass and backcloth showing
A day of unity and understanding, to end remorse.

Whose hand on the tiller?
Whose hand on the wheel?
Only divine power and not a sinner
Will plan true love's course as real.
She grips my arm and I hear her sigh,
I see the twinkle of a rainbow in her eye.
Her action is clear and the seeds are sown.
She whispers very gently, 'Let's go home.'

Ernest S Peaford

GIFTS ALL AROUND

For these great gifts I thank Thee -
The glowing fire
Which cheers the hearts of men
And lifts the gloom of winter days.

Water, running clear and fresh
Beneath the earth
And welling up to quench our thirst.

And the freshening earth,
Which nourishes the seeds
Till harvest time.

Great Father, all around we see Thy works
Of power and beauty
Let us learn to give Thee thanks
For all Thy precious gifts to help mankind.

Marcella Pellow

AMEN

God is a myth, a spirit force,
He is the mind of the universe,
Created all there will be, here forever,
Does, makes all, space and planets together

Shattered to fragments, after making time
Each having perception, and feelings sublime
Each tiny piece has know-how of whole,
To unite to one godhead, an almighty soul.

Sundays has church, is full of good-living people,
Thousands of churches, some priests in robes,
Think good thoughts, they sing and they pray,
Only good receiver would know what they say.

The going to church, and dressed in the best,
At least once a week, you're clean, well-dressed,
I am sure going to church, is good for the soul,
Don't cost a lot, few bob in a bowl.

The teaching is built, around the word Love
If there is a God or not, below or above,
If we all held fast, as strong as steel rods,
And all loved each other, all could be gods.

The skies around us are filled to capacity,
With gas and rock, held with tenacity
So far away, farther than light's speedy flight
We don't understand, we haven't the sight.

H Cotterill

THE BLOOMS WERE THERE TO REMIND ME

A stranger brought me lovely blooms,
such a bright array.
They came when I was feeling low
and blew my blues away.

Methinks I saw in the display
a rainbow bright and clear.
After the sorrow I felt joyous
and felt the Lord so near.

I thanked God for the flowers
that a stranger brought my way.
They told me God was close by me,
and close by me to stay.

The blossoms held the message,
to me so very clear.
They were a sweet and kind reminder
that the Lord is always near.
                    Of course!

Rosie Hues

UNTITLED

If there is a Time to come
As there was a time that's passed:

Will I laugh as I did then
Thoughtless of the time ahead?

Will these limbs once strong and fleet
Leap once more at my command?

Will I love as deep and true?
As I once did long ago?

Will the thoughts I shared with friends?
Spring again, again, again?

Will the people that I cherished
Rise again to bring me joy?

Will the children, mine amongst them
Dance beneath my vine and sing?

Will the God who gave me being
Bear me in His arms once more?

If there is a Time to come
As there was a time that's passed,

Grant, Oh Lord, at its beginning
That there may be peace at last.

C D Isherwood

My Thanks

Thank you Lord for this world of ours
The mountains, the trees and the beautiful flowers,
Thank you for the birds that sing all day,
And little children at their play.

Thanks for the river, sea and stream,
And for the grass, so rich and green,
Thanks for the friends we meet each day
And the many blessings that come our way.

Thanks for our homes, and loved ones there,
Who tend to us with such loving care,
Thanks for the moon, the stars and sun,
And the bed where we rest when day is done,
For all these blessings, our thanks to Thee
May we ever grateful be.

Amelia Roberts

HARBOROUGH 2999

Standing on Roman Way
In near pitch-blackness
Church of St Dionysius spire just visible
No cars or people or taxis.

I use a torch to find my way
To the church to go inside
I enter the candlelit house of the Lord
From the dark and cold I seek to hide.

I look at my watch it's New Year's Eve
2999 Tuesday nearly midnight
A priest explains how 'Global Warming'
Had moved the Gulf Stream out of right.

Our winters had become much colder,
And our summers much, much wetter
England's population has fallen sharp
No one knows when things will get better.

New Year's Day, Wednesday 1/1/3000
All the buildings covered in ice
People in bearskins and other skins for warmth
Because the car is king in 2001, not very nice.

H Griffiths

Easter

Easter is a lovely time
Church bells ring
Hymns will be sung
Cards will be sent
To those far and near
With Easter eggs large and small
Shapes and sizes, for one and all
With daffodils all about, and
All sorts of other spring flowers out
Can't we think of a better time
When Easter time comes around
So if we believe a little
We must say a prayer
As Jesus must have suffered
On that cross so bare.

Doreen Day

THE MEANING OF SPRING

What do we mean when we call it 'spring',
When all around us life is springing?
Can it be true that on swallow's wing
Persephone her gifts is bringing?
From earliest days men have perceived
Life out of death some hand is flinging
Riches untold to man and beast,
Setting their thankful voices singing.

The Giver men called by many names,
Age after age in knowledge growing,
Watching the seed that lifeless seemed
Wake to reward their trustful sowing.
Yet still some sacrifice, they felt,
Yearly must set the magic flowing.
Dimly they sought, as best they could,
A way to repay what they were owing.

In latter days we've grown so clever,
Forgetting faith that made men wise
Until grim evil strikes, and never
Had we more need to use our eyes.
See how our greed has urged us ever
Bigger, not better, ways to devise
The making use of fellow creatures -
That way, be sure, disaster lies.

So as each year draws on to Easter
Still grows our hope that, drop by drop,
Like children engaged in foolish quarrel,
When mothers' support will be our prop,
We learnt, from childish insults uttered,
Hoping they'd bring us out on top -
'He did it first,' enraged we muttered
Came answer, 'Then you be first to stop.'

Kathleen M Hatton

The Coming Of Christ

With bated breath in the Heavenly heights
Smiled holy angels in delight.
'Tis true then of the news we hear
That a Prince be born of this holy sphere
Give signs to mortals let them rejoice
A Saviour to save them 'tis God's choice.

Upon Earth news spread far and wide
The Son of God is coming people cried
'Tis written in the scriptures, the prophets said
Also the learned and the well-read.

God revealed to Mary that it was she
Who was chosen for the Holy Mother to be
For me you will give birth to my sacred son
Who will be the light of life for everyone.
Joseph, Mary's betrothed standing by her side
Accepted this news humbled, honoured and with pride.

When the birthing time was right
Heavenly spheres shone diamond bright
And a stillness enclosed the Earth
Whilst in a stable with just straw for a cradle
Holy Mary did give birth.

A Saviour was born as predicted you see
To save all sinners where'er they may be
Heaven and Earth rejoiced as one
As wise, learned men nodded and said 'Tis done.'

Brenda Killingback

BE STILL

Be still my restless heart. Let go!
Unleash the troubles and worries.
They're traps that bind the spirit so
Anxiety comes in flurries,
Depressing and leaving one low.

Be still my restless heart and soul.
Muted prayer, unformed, unspoken
Begs the Lord, his help to enrol
Saved from darkness, to be woken
To silence. A balm that makes whole.

Be still my heart. Be still. Calm down.
Tune to the rhythm of the waves.
Let go the fears, the pain and frown,
The peace and quiet that you crave
Waits to be nurtured and full-grown.

Be still, at rest on the Lord's arm.
Remember that His every lamb
He guards and protects from all harm.
Each a part of his precious plan
As he informs us in the Psalm.

Be still, Be still and fear not.
In His presence be still. Be calm!

Kathleen Potter

THE LORD'S GIFT

Please Lord protect them
        day and night,
And keep them safe
        until daylight,
As babies are your gift to us.

We'll do our best to
        keep them warm,
And keep them safe
        from all harm,
As we know babies are a gift.

We'll feed them well
        until they're strong,
And try to teach them
        right from wrong,
We know they are a precious gift.

Then one day when
        they're fully grown,
They'll go out into
        the world alone,
We know this gift was only on loan.

Ann Ogilvie

MY DAILY PRAYER

Thank you, Father, for all your care,
Wherever I am I know you are there.
Please keep my loved ones safe from harm;
When trials arise, may I stay calm.
You know the needs of all who are ill,
Help those who care to do your will.
Our life is but a fleeting day,
Thank you, Father, for the time to pray.

Joan Picton

SAFE HOME AT EVENTIDE

Dear Lord of all the universe
Look down on me today
To guide my faltering footsteps
In the straight and narrow way.
Reach out and take my hand
Holding it close in Thine
That I might know that every day
Thy love dear Lord is mine.

Oh walk close beside me
In case I lose my way
Lead me though the darkness
Be my strength and stay.
Where Thou leadest I will follow
With Thee to be my guide
I cannot fail to arrive dear Lord
Safe home at eventide.

Mary Ferguson

THAT BETTER PART

Did you hear that still, small voice
Deep within your heart,
You are privileged to be chosen
To take that 'better part'.

To find a place of safety
A place with food and sun
Rooted in love all evil force
With strength is truly shun.

We may have come from other folds
Our place we long to find
To grow and flourish in the peace
With those of our own kind.

We know our Heavenly Father
Alert to every breeze
A jealous watch He keeps
Of space, providing all our needs.

As a priceless pearl by sand
And sea is shaped
Much more to God when fully grown
We stand in beauty draped.

Olive Bedford

INNOCENT EYES

The world through a child's eyes is an innocent place,
Where people live together happily - the human race
There is no discrimination against creed or colour,
Just content and happy to be with each other.

They greet each day bright and new,
In their small world, troubles are few.
No war, no fighting or hating mankind
Only love and happiness will we find.

What a wonderful picture they do paint
Of a perfect world without a flaw or taint
A world full of love, trust and respect,
So open, so honest and so direct.

Our world could be a wonderful place,
Living happily together - the human race.
No conflict, hatred or bitter lies,
If we could only view the world through those innocent eyes.

Susan Revell

A Goodnight Prayer

Thank you Lord for the passing day
Your loving presence ever near me
Forgive what I did wrong or failed to do
In showing my love for You.
Guard my dear ones, help those in need
Let me show them your love in every deed
Give me a quiet sleep I pray
Greeting the new day with you, dear Lord
To lighten my way.

Elisabeth Morley

LIVE IN PEACE

Lord I pray for all those in need
Who want you to answer
At their own speed
Lend them Lord, your listening ear
Help them, understand
Your timing so, that they lose their fear.

It's not your will
That they should suffer,
But you are not, a spiritual buffer,
We should be speaking to you each day.
And learning about life
Jesus' way.

You don't desert us, when in trouble
But, you act through your mercy, on the double.
It may not be the way
We view our need
In our misery Lord
Aid us to succeed.
Because you Lord, see and know, how we fall,
And continue to act in love, towards one and all.

It's for the world to trust
You Father, more and more,
You don't want to see, bloodshed or war
We need to look to you
Every day
And lead our lives
Your kind of way.

So thank you Heavenly
Father above,
Watch over us
Showing your brand of love.

Louise White

POETIC PRAYERS

Please bless all those in need
Every colour, race and creed
Because they need your love indeed
And the will to succeed.

Please bless everyone in pain
And may they come to know
Just how much you really care
And how much you love them so.

May everyone in torment
Come to love you and repent
For each and every sin
And show all the love they have within.

Janet Larkin

Chaos

Chaos! . . . Chaos! . . . All was lost
The man who died upon the cross
Had robbed me of my faith it seemed
Through my alcoholic dreams
My God you have forsaken me
Oblivious to what might be
A lesson he was learning me?
But Why? Why me a strong believer
Born to be.
. . . Many a year and to the day
I remember how I knelt to pray
And shouted loud yes! Loud to Him
Am I paying the price for some sort of sin?
Please put me on the road to sobriety
I'm not a drinker
This is not me! . . .
He did!
The warmth I felt surround me
Really *did* astound me
He really *was* there tho I could not see
I *felt* the change come over me
No more whisky, no more gin - and
That's the day I packed it all in.

Pearls

ON HIGH

True meaning of, the Christmas time
With hopes of joy begun,
God alone, to come on Earth,
In shape of precious Son,
It was, a test of people's faith,
Their hopes on high restore,
Would last throughout the coming years,
For prayers to God, implore.
When Mary heard from angel o'er
On how, the birth, to be,
How this should see, that Virgin I,
But what you've said, be done, to me.
So the Holy Spirit, descended from above,
To cover Mary, with his love,
The babe was born, no room at inn,
Instead, a humble stable,
Mary, Joseph there, with ox and ass,
The birth, did be, enable,
The three wise men, had heard of birth,
And wished, to give their gifts,
Were guided by the star on high
Until it came to rest,
Up above where Jesus lay,
Long journey had them stressed,
When sleep came o'er, wise men, had dream,
And told go other way,
Away from Herod
As false, were of his worships day.

Hugh Campbell

EVER PRESENT

You come to us in good times
Stay with us through the bad
Who could ask any more of you
No better ally we could ever have,
The way we sometimes act
Must make you shake your head in wonder
Ever since you gave us choices
We have made blunder after blunder,
Still you are ever present
Only you can tell us why
Hope all our family's included
When it's our turn to pass by
We have every faith in you
You are our world's greatest gift
Whenever our spirit weakens
We can rely on you to assist,
Whatever the problem
No matter how large or small
Our Lord as always is with us
To save us from the fall.

T Butler

TO YOU I PRAY

Dear Father, hear me, as I pray to you this night.
For peace, throughout the world.
Food for the starving people, where there is famine and drought.
For our own people who have suffered with devastating floods,
And our farmers who have lost their livelihoods
through disease amongst their cattle - some of generations of breeding.
Bless the nurses and doctors in our surgeries and hospitals,
who go about helping the sick and lonely and the dying.
Rest your healing hands on the sick,
to comfort them in their hours of pain, when they need you most.
People who live alone, need your presence
during the dark hours of night.
Give them your peace to understand your love for them.
We have heard the Christmas story of a baby, born in a stable
and visited by shepherds and kings. A baby born to be a king.
Now as Easter time draws near we hear another story.
A very poignant one of love, hate, denial and death on a cross.
We will celebrate the Last Supper in our churches,
and Communion on Easter Day with the risen Lord.
Such a joyous day.
Our church ministers need your help to preach the message of your
good news to all people.
Help us to understand all your promises and your love for us.
Be with the homeless who live on the streets, some through no fault
of their own. Show them the right way to go. They need you.
Bless all our loved ones who have gone before,
to live with you, in your Kingdom.
We still miss them and know that one day, we will meet again.

Joan Smith

SOUNDS OF TEMPTATION

Sheathed in coldness
Like a splinter of ice,
The Son prepares to die.

Man's ploughing self
On some far away hill
Forgets His cross,

Flowers of snow
And muffled scents
Hide the treason.

In a thicket of thorns
The bell of sin tolls on
With its deadly ransom.

Marylène Walker

WORDS OF GOLD

Words of gold
Are seldom sold.
A diamond ring
Is a very rare thing.

Respect is due
Where words are true.
Where love inspires
Romance never tires.

Prayer for two
Is sweet to do:
Sorrows to share
With useful care.

Grace transmutes pain
Preparing to reign
Above the starry dome
In our final home.

John Rae Walker

THE REPLY

The widow speaks
'Fifty years of love and laughter,
And all that is left
Is a handful of ashes in a wooden box
Buried in the ground,
And bitter-sweet memories.'

The husband replies
'Dearest,
Love and laughter are from God,
And cannot be destroyed.
As the seed dies to produce an apple tree,
A thing of usefulness and beauty for God,
So the body dies and the soul
Grows with beauty and usefulness for God.
One day when you're worn out body dies,
We will be closer than we were before
Wrapped in the wondrous mantle of God's love.'

J B Allan

The Heritage

My garden, my Shangri-La,
My Heaven on Earth,
Created, by God who gave it birth.

The trees in their spring, summer
Autumn and winter dress,
Given to us by God, to love and caress.
What magic he waves with the flowers in bloom,
While the birds flying by trilling out a sweet tune.

Oh God how I feel you so deep in my heart,
Please how I beg you don't ever depart,
Let's try to give comfort to those who don't understand
Just reach out with a smile and a comforting hand
Now God looking down from His Heavenly throne,
Stretched out his arms, one day my children you'll all come home.

Just remember you reap what you sow
May the seeds that you scatter with such love and such care,
Reach out to your loved ones as they flow through the air.

Marie Stanton

A Circle With No End

A circle with no end
A rotating sphere with no meaning or way to defend.
Dots on the landscape scurrying by
Making no sense of that so enigmatic question 'Why?'
No start, no end, as the arc becomes one,
A tunnel so dark and unknown.
An electrifying light; our journey begun.
A life so precious; yet not for keeps, only on loan.
Until, as the arc rotates, the tunnel emerges,
Oh so white.
All is clarified; the magnet draws us -
We've fought our last fight.
Continuation - a circle with no end.

M A Shipp Yule

PSALM 121 - THE LORD OUR PROTECTOR

I look to the mountains,
Where will my help come from,
He who made Heaven and Earth,
Moon and the stars and sun.

The sun will not hurt you,
During the time of light,
The moon will not hurt you,
During the time of night.

He will not let you fall,
Our protector will guide us all,
He will guard us all,
Guard against the wall.

From danger you will be safe,
During the working day,
Now and forever more,
These are the words we pray.

He will not let you fall,
Our protector will guide us all,
He will guard us all,
Guard against the wall.

John Cook

TURNING AROUND

F inding the words to apologise
O r learning just to compromise.
R eaching out to help another
G iving a hand to your brother.
I nnumerable paths show
V aluable new routes to go.
I ncreasing tolerance all around
N egotiating the neutral ground.
G iving for so altering the trends
   as
       Forgiving does by making amends.

H D Hensman

LOST IN WONDER, LOVE AND PRAISE...

Blood-red sunsets, blush-pink dawns,
Soaring buzzards, diving hawks,
Rowdy rooks and laughing jays -
Will never cease but to amaze.

Deep scored valleys, mountain peaks,
Rolling hills and lofty crags,
Waving crops and swaying trees -
My spirit soars at sight of these.

Silent snow and crackling ice,
Jagged lightning, drenching storms,
Bouncing hail and rumbling thunder -
All bring me to the point of wonder.

Wispy mist and blanket fog,
Echoing caverns, sunken lakes,
Crashing waves and shimmering sand -
How mighty is the Maker's hand.

Scuttling rabbits, running deer,
Shady woods and bubbling becks,
Drifting clouds and clear, blue sky -
I'll praise the Lord until I die.

And then beyond this earthly life,
Above all trauma, toil and strife,
Whate'er is found in heavenly rest
Will better be - in faith, the best.

David Varley

TRUTH'S VISION

To be afraid and unsure
To face that final curtain
Is to look truth in the face
Of that I am certain

To have that empty feeling
To know you stand alone
Is to look truth in the face
And for your sins atone

To be beset by worries
To feel cast out and frail
Is to look truth in the face
Before your soul sets sail

To stand alone and upright
To hear that clarion call
Is to look truth in the face
As you enter into His hall

To meet at last your Maker
And know that you are blest
Is to reach that final truth
And know you are at rest.

Margaret Gurney

Dear Lord! Is It Me?

Some people are sent to this Earth
With talents galore - right from birth
They can write verse and prose
Or even dance on their toes
Dear Lord, what happened to me?

Some people can roll up their sleeves
Get 'stuck in' with oh so much ease
The things that they touch
Can please others so much
Dear Lord, why can't it be me?

Some people can knit, paint or sew
Others make beautiful flowers grow
Some can sing with such ease
Or do good works on their knees
Dear Lord, I wish it was me.

Some people give time for a while
To try and make other folk smile
Perhaps ease their pain
Make them feel whole again
Dear Lord, please let it be me.

Some people whose talents are gone
Because time is ticking along
Are so thankful for friends
On whose help they depend
Dear Lord, I know it is me.

B Hayman

The Things That I See

As I look in your eyes, your deep, brown eyes,
I see all the things that have made you cry.
All the happiness that you have known in your life,
Plus all of the sadness and all of the strife.

I see memories of days so full of light,
The times the sun faded and left you with night.
Visions you will recall forever and a day,
The times you chose to look away.

As I look in your eyes - I see dreams come true.
All of the wishes your heart still clings to.
Friends and loved ones who have come and gone.
Holding dear the advice that they passed on.

I can see your whole lifetime - the good and the bad,
What made you happy and what made you sad.
As I look in your eyes, I can see what you've seen,
All that you've done - all that you've been.

Helen Riley

MUSIC OF THE FLOWER GARDEN

The song of the canary bird,
The ringing of Canterbury bells,
Soft melodies of mimulus,
An ocean's echo in crocus shells.

The harmonies of dianthus blended
With the rock-rock beat of the Alpine crowd,
And howls of juvenile poppies,
Colour-chaotic, loud.

The clamour of roses to besiege
Us with beauty every day,
The whistle of lilies emerging
From the scattered chords of May.

Tinkling tips of golden thyme,
The breathlessness of grass,
The cry of the chrysanthemum
As the best days pass.

This is how the flower garden
Sings for us its story - no
Chorus more joyous - pop song
To oratorio!

Nigel M Chisholm

BEAUTY IS...

Beauty is the miracle of each newborn babes birth
Beauty is the seed that grows from within the earth
Beauty is the flower that opens to greet each morn
Beauty is the sunset that arrives to meet each new dawn
Beauty is the animals and the wonders of the world
Beauty is the song sung from every kind of bird
Beauty is the love which is given freely all around
Beauty is serenity look within and it is found
Beauty is found within silence not a sound
Beauty is the still, dark of the night
Beauty is each new day bringing with it the daylight
Beauty is the spirit when it leaves to go to a higher place
Beauty is the memory of a loved one's kind and loving face.

Elizabeth Leach

Magical Woodland

Sunset fades towards the west
Draped in deep vermilion vest,
The skies then darken to midnight blue,
And the moon and stars arise in silver hue

They cast their nightly magic,
Upon the world below,
As the woodlands begin to rustle,
And, the crystal rivers flow.

The song thrush sings his serenade,
Symbolic of the flute,
And high above the woodland floor
The owl is heard with its deep, resonant hoot.

Spiders webs like fairies wings,
Adorning trees do shimmer,
And deep amongst the hedges
Glow-worm lamps do glimmer.

The earth erupts a nose pops out,
A velvet mole appears to look about,
Hidden in the grass a lonely cricket sings,
And suddenly, across the pathway a startled grasshopper springs.

Moths fly upwards to the sky,
Attracted by the light
Sonic sounds from bats are heard,
All creatures of the night.

Comfy in our beds we sleep,
Relieved the day has passed,
But deep beneath the woodland,
A magic spell is being cast.

Lynda Fordham

MY DAUGHTER

All things bright and beautiful,
It is such a lovely song
It reminds me of my daughter
On the day she came along.

As a little girl I would watch her play
So much pleasure she gave to me
And the comfort of her little soul
As she sat upon my knee.

I could see the brightness in her eyes
The fire-red colour in her hair
A gift of beauty sent to me
Along with her love and care.

She has grown up now and gone away
And I hope one day I'll see
That our dear Lord sends her a gift
And has all the pleasures just like me.

A F Mace

THINGS I LOVE IN GOD'S WORLD

I love majestic mountains,
I love the valleys green;
And crystal sparkling fountains,
The purest ever seen;
And wild and rugged country
Has always thrilled me so;
Its wild and untamed beauty
Stays with me, e'er I go.

I love the bright, warm sunshine,
I feel its heat-kissed glow;
And crisp, bright winter mornings,
With crisp, white, sparkling snow.
Love leaping lambs in springtime,
I love a waterfall;
I love to hear church bells chime,
I praise God for them all.

I love wide, open spaces,
The windswept moorland fell;
Love happy, smiling faces,
Their inner joy they tell;
Love bright, exotic flowers
And brightly coloured birds;
Love soft, refreshing showers,
And Nordic reindeer herds.

I love to travel widely
Throughout God's wondrous world;;
I love to view His wonders -
Creation's scene unfurled.
I've seen wildlife of Africa,
And wide majestic fjords;
The snow-capped peaks of Austria;
This Earth is *all* the Lord's.

Irene Hart

SUMMER TIME

Intoxicating sun, with air
That wafts the strong perfume
Of honeysuckle, rambler rose
And other plants in bloom.

The countryside displays its wealth,
As flowers now abound,
Their brilliant kaleidoscopes
Are scattered all around.

On holiday we have the time
To gaze at many things,
To marvel at the butterflies'
Fine patterns on their wings.

Beyond the bracken's curling fronds
Appears the rippling sea,
So blue beneath the summer sky,
It flows enticingly.

We hasten now along the cliff
Until we reach our cove,
To plunge once more into the waves,
For this is what we love.

Refreshed, we wade onto the sand,
Soft warmth beneath our feet,
The ocean's treasures lying there:
Its shells so bright and neat.

From morning, noon until the dusk
We spend our days sublime
Relaxing in the open air,
Enjoying summertime.

Anne Greenhow

THE RAINBOW

Iridescent, ethereal, horseshoe-shaped arc,
Rose, orange, yellow making their mark.
Green, blue, indigo, violet complete the bow,
Rain and sunshine, reflect and glow.
One of God's miracles, radiantly show.
Ephemeral, transient, soul-raising span
God's promise to Noah, God's promise to Man.

Jane Finlayson

SPRINGTIME

When it's springtime in the garden
And grey skies begin to clear
The trees burst out in blossom
It's my favourite time of year

The crocus and the snowdrop
Are the first to show their heads
The daffodils and tulips
Soon cover flower beds

The dawn chorus from the treetops
Wake me early every day
The birds will soon be nesting
In the hedgerows along the way

When I'm digging in the garden
Round the roses that I tend
The robin isn't far away
He is the gardeners friend

The song thrush and the blackbird
The butterfly and the bee
Will the blue tit use the nest box
That I fixed to the willow tree?

The season that new life begins
For fledglings, lambs and cubs
When mother feeds her baby birds
On aphids, worms and grubs

But don't forget the frog spawn
From tadpoles they will grow
The farmer in his fields again
Wheat and corn he will sow

So make the most of springtime
Early flowers soon disappear
Enjoy the gifts of our good Lord
It's my favourite time of year.

Tom Rutherford

THERE IS A TIME

There is a time, so we are told
when riches spill and joys unfold,
when secrets inner wisdom speaks,
sometimes loud, sometimes weak, oblique.

This time is now so I am told,
and if I listen, then the gold
will be revealed, like drops of myrrh,
into myself they will inter.

Heart awake, third eye shutter open wide,
peace within, the channel's clear, allied
to time and space. I ask for aid.
The sound is clear, the Love's relayed.

There is a light beyond the hill,
opening out, yet peaceful still,
and in that Light a Presence speaks,
not loud, not soft, and not oblique.

No word is heard and yet I know
The joy which is relayed,
comes to me with Blessings great,
to pass to others through the Gate.

The Great Gate of Life, as it
unfolds, and hands reach out
in healing blessing to those who need
the Channel growing bright indeed.

My thanks then for the source of light
that keeps my channel burning bright.
May I thus keep pure and clear
the Image of the Saviour here.

Jeni Merrifield

THANKFULNESS

Lord, we come to Thee
With humble, thankful hearts
For the freedom to link with Thee in loving fellowship
and to ask for Thy protection and guidance - in our everyday lives.
We give thanks for the many blessings of spirit
And for the food we eat also the loving, safe homes.
We ask that we have the strength and purpose of the Master, Christ
In all we do to bring light and love to those in darkness and need.

Julia L Holden

WONDROUS LOVE

I looked at his face in wonderment
brimmed to the top with joy,
the features finely balanced
of this beautiful, baby boy.

He came into this world of ours
weighed in at nine pound one,
fair of hair and eyes so blue
they capture everyone.

They say he has his mother's mouth
his father's eyes and ears,
seeing this babe new to this world
filled me full to tears.

Beholding this joy, this gift of life
a great blessing from above,
we rejoice in our baby Jacob
who fills us with wondrous love.

Wendy Ann Lively

INFORMATION

We hope you have enjoyed reading this book - and that you will continue to enjoy it in the coming years.

If you like reading and writing poetry drop us a line, or give us a call, and we'll send you a free information pack.

Write to :-
**Triumph House Information
Remus House
Coltsfoot Drive
Peterborough
PE2 9JX
(01733) 898102**